The Good Parenting Food Guide

Jane Ogden

The Good Parenting Food Guide

Managing What Children Eat without Marking Food a Problem

WILEY Blackwell

Registered Office
John Wiley & Sons Ltd, The Atrium, Southern Gate, Chichester, West Sussex, PO19 8SQ, UK

Editorial Offices
350 Main Street, Malden, MA 02148-5020, USA
9600 Garsington Road, Oxford, OX4 2DQ, UK
The Atrium, Southern Gate, Chichester, West Sussex, PO19 8SQ, UK

For details of our global editorial offices, for customer services, and for information about how to apply for permission to reuse the copyright material in this book please see our website at www.wiley.com/wiley-blackwell.

Library of Congress Cataloging-in-Publication data is available for this book.

ISBN 9781118741894 (hardback); ISBN 9781118709375 (paperback)

A catalogue record for this book is available from the British Library.

Cover images: From top: © BestPhotoStudio / Shutterstock; photo © Andrew Peart; © Wavebreakmedia / Shutterstock; © Sofarina79 / Shutterstock; photo © Andrew Peart; © Fotofreaks / Shutterstock
Cover design by Cyan Design

Set in 10.5/13 pt Minion Pro-Regular by Toppan Best-set Premedia Limited
Printed and bound in Malaysia by Vivar Printing Sdn Bhd

1   2014

For Harry and Ellie who have taught me everything I know about being a parent.

One thing is certain: if we stay the same, nothing around us is likely to change very much. So if we're hoping for changes in the family, we may need to start with ourselves. Let's get started! (Candida Hunt and Annette Mountford, 2003. *The Parenting Puzzle. The Family Links Nurturing Programme.* Oxford: Family Links)

Contents

Introduction

Feeding children should be easy. Hunger is a basic biological drive and eating should be a straightforward and fun part of family life. But so often it is not. Parents are busy, food is expensive and cooking takes time, and even when you have managed to prepare the family meal, children announce random likes and dislikes that seem to come out of nowhere. And on top of all that, we have the fears of obesity and eating disorders looming in the background. How do we get our children to eat healthily when they don't like healthy food? How do we get them to eat more without making them fat? How do we keep them a normal weight without giving them an eating disorder? How do we get them to be more active when all they want to do is watch TV or play on their phone? And what do we do about a daughter who starts to obsess about her weight?

This book aims to describe what constitutes a healthy diet and how to achieve this without making food an issue for your child. It addresses many of the problems parents face when feeding their children and offers tips on how to overcome these without making matters worse. And it looks at the ways in which we talk about food, shop and prepare food, and eat food with our children, and the impact this has on them as they grow up.

Who Is It For?

This book is aimed at parents with children across the age range from babies and toddlers through to teenagers and young adults. Some may feel they have a specific problem with feeding their child, but many may just want to know how to bring their children up to have a healthy approach to eating. The book could also be used by health visitors, nurses, GPs, dieticians, and nutritionists who need extra information or want a resource to recommend to their patients.

The Author

I am a Professor in Health Psychology at the University of Surrey and have carried out research in the area of eating behavior, food preferences, obesity, and eating disorders for 25 years. I also teach psychologists, dieticians, nutritionists, and medical students about how we learn to like the food we like and how eating is about so much more than just hunger and fullness. I have published over 140 papers and five books, two of which focus specifically on eating behavior. These are *Fat Chance! The Myth of Dieting Explained* and *The Psychology of Eating: From Healthy to Disordered Behavior*. In addition, I have published several articles in magazines and often contribute to health discussions on the radio, television, and in magazines and newspapers.

I also have two children now aged 14 and 11.

This book is the end result of 25 years of knowing the theory and doing research into eating behavior and 14 years of working out how on earth to put it into practice. My motto for parenting is "Aim high, then when you slither into a pit you have further to fall." My motto for food is "Try to give your child a healthy diet. But try even harder NOT to give them a problem with food." This book is about managing that middle ground when you have aimed high but life has added in a good dose of slither. It is also about managing what your child eats without making food an issue.

The Structure of the Book

The book is in two halves. The first half covers facts and theories and the second describes tips and reality. Ideally I would like all readers to start at the beginning and read straight through. But if you don't have the time (or inclination) to do this, there are "take home points" for each chapter in the first half and "what do we know" and "what can we do" catch-up points for the second half.

Facts and theories

This section consists of eight chapters which describe the facts and theories about eating and its related problems. First, it describes healthy eating in terms of what is healthy for different age groups, and why a healthy diet is important in both childhood and later life, and it looks at who actually eats a healthy diet. The next two chapters then focus on how we learn to like the food we eat and the role food plays in our lives. They describe the impact of simple familiarity, the role of learning from others, and the associations we make between food, social situations, and our mood. I then highlight how food has many meanings beyond hunger and fullness which influence what and how much we eat. This section then describes how eating behavior is a habit, and why habits are so hard to change, and it offers some general ways in which habits can be broken. The next four chapters look at eating problems, with a focus on obesity and eating disorders. They describe how common these problems are, their causes, how they can be prevented, and possible treatments. They also cover how some of the strategies used to treat obesity and eating disorders can be used at home.

Tips and reality

This section consists of six chapters and takes a much more practical approach, offering some simple tips for managing some of the problems with parenting and food. These are all grounded in the facts and theories given in the first section and, I hope, illustrate how they can be turned into practice. This section addresses the following problems:

- "I don't have time to cook"
- "My child won't eat a healthy diet"
- "My child watches too much TV"
- "My child eats too much"
- "My child won't eat enough"
- "My child thinks they are fat"

I have also put together some simple recipes for family meals that take very little time and effort (really!), help you keep your sanity, and are always healthier than ready meals or takeaways. These are in the chapter on cooking (Chapter 9).

Finally, the last chapter pulls together some of the key ideas of the book and offers some final take home points.

A Note on Language

I am a mum and for the last 14 years of my life have lived in a world of mums at toddler groups, the school gate, sports days, and the local park. In my world it is still mums who do most of the day-to-day parenting of their children and worry about whether or not they are doing a good job. I am fully aware that times are changing and that, out there, many men are stepping up to the task in hand. In fact we have one full-time house dad at my daughter's school and I take my hat off to him as he seems to have all the effort without some of the rewards of chat and friendship. So in this book I often say "mums" when I really mean "the parent in charge." I hope this doesn't alienate dads. It is not meant to at all. It just reflects the world that I see and those who I expect will be most interested in reading this book.

A Note on Detail

I am an academic and most of my writing is for academic papers and people who do research. The aim of this book is to make this research interesting and accessible to busy parents. I have therefore tried to include enough detail to be useful but not too much detail, which can be boring. If you want any further information then please use the recommended reading and reference lists at the end of the book. Please also read my more academic book on eating behavior: *The Psychology of Eating: From Healthy to Disordered Behavior*, 2nd edition, published by Wiley Blackwell in 2010.

Acknowledgments

I am grateful to the following mums who gave me their feedback on an earlier draft of this book and, I hope, helped me pitch it at the right level: Frances Brewer, Anne Neale, Liz Paoli, Anne Peart, Sarah Richardson, and Melanie Simcox.

The photos are taken by David Armstrong, Jane Ogden, Ellie Ogden, and Harry Ogden.

Facts and theories

1

What is healthy eating?

Magazines, newspapers, and radio and TV programs are full of articles and items about the importance of a healthy diet and what a healthy diet actually is. Often this information is confusing and sometimes it is wrong. This chapter attempts to clarify the world of healthy eating and will describe:

- A brief history of healthy eating
- Healthy eating in the modern day
- Healthy eating throughout childhood
- Why a healthy diet is important

A Brief History of Healthy Eating

The nature of a good diet has changed dramatically over the years. In 1824 *The Family Oracle of Good Health* published in the UK recommended that young ladies should eat the following at breakfast: "plain biscuit (not bread), broiled beef steaks or mutton chops, under done without any fat and half a pint of bottled ale, the genuine Scots ale is the best"; or if this was too strong, it suggested "one small breakfast cup of good strong tea or of coffee – weak tea or coffee is always bad for the nerves as well as the complexion." Dinner is later described as similar to breakfast, with "no vegetables, boiled meat, no made dishes being permitted much less fruit, sweet things or

The Good Parenting Food Guide: Managing What Children Eat without Making Food a Problem, First Edition. Jane Ogden.
© 2014 John Wiley & Sons, Ltd. Published 2014 by John Wiley & Sons, Ltd.

Good parenting . . .

A healthy diet is important for how a child grows and develops. It also helps children stay healthy once they are adults as many adult illnesses start in childhood long before we have any symptoms. Good parenting is therefore about helping your child to eat a healthy diet and to develop good eating habits. It is also about making food nice without it being an issue.

pastry . . . the steaks and chops must always be the chief part of your food." In the 1840s Dr Kitchener recommended in his diet book a lunch of "a bit of roasted poultry, a basin of good beef tea, eggs poached . . . a sandwich – stale bread – and half a pint of good home brewed beer" (1). In the US at this time, diets were based around the staples of corn, rye, oats, and barley for making bread, the use of molasses as a cheap sweetener, and a quantity of salt pork, which could survive the warmer weather in the absence of refrigeration. Blood pudding was also a source of meat; it was made from hog or occasionally beef blood and chopped pork, seasoned and stuffed into a casing which was eaten with butter crackers to provide a meal for the workers. What constituted a healthy diet in the nineteenth century was very different from current recommendations.

Most improvements in the diets of many Western countries mainly came about as a result of the rationing imposed during both the world wars. These rations resulted in a reduction in the consumption of sweet foods and an increase in the role of carbohydrate in the diet. In addition, the need to provide the armed forces with safe and healthy food stimulated research into food technology and established dietary standards.

Healthy Eating in the Modern Day

Over the past 30 years there has been a proliferation of literature on healthy eating. A visit to any bookstore will reveal shelves of books full of diets designed to improve health through weight management, salt reduction, a Mediterranean approach to eating, or the consumption of fiber. Nowadays there is, however, a consensus among nutritionists as to what constitutes a healthy diet (2). Descriptions of healthy eating tend to divide food into broad food groups and make recommendations as to the relative consumption of each of these groups. Recommendations change across the lifespan as we grow from babies into toddlers, to children, to teenagers, then adults. They even change as adults get older, as we need different diets at different stages, such as pregnancy, the menopause and as we progress into older adulthood. Current recommendations for children aged over 5 and for adults are the same, and are outlined below. These are:

- **Fruit and vegetables**: A wide variety of fruit and vegetables should be eaten, and preferably five or more servings should be eaten per day.
- **Bread, pasta, other cereals, and potatoes**: Plenty of complex carbohydrate foods should be eaten, preferably those high in fiber such as brown bread, brown pasta, and brown rice.
- **Meat, fish, and alternatives**: Moderate amounts of meat, fish, and alternatives should be eaten and it is recommended that the low-fat varieties are chosen.
- **Milk and dairy products**: These should be eaten in moderation, and the low-fat alternatives should be chosen where possible.
- **Fatty and sugary foods**: Food such as potato chips, sweets, and sugary drinks should be consumed infrequently and in small amounts.

Other recommendations for adults include a moderate intake of alcohol (a maximum of 3–4 units per day for men and 2–3 units per day for women), the consumption of fluoridated water where possible, a limited salt intake of 6 g per day, eating unsaturated fats from olive oil and oily fish rather than saturated fats from butter and margarine, and consuming complex carbohydrates (e.g. bread and pasta) rather than simple carbohydrates (e.g. sugar). It is also recommended that men aged between 19 and 59 consume about 2,550 calories per day and that similarly aged women consume about 1,920 calories per day, although this depends on body size and degree of physical activity.

Recommendations for children are less restrictive for fatty foods and dairy products, and it is suggested that parents should not restrict the fat intake of children aged under 2. By 5 years old, however, children should be consuming a diet similar to that recommended for adults, which is high in complex carbohydrates such as brown bread, brown pasta, and brown rice, high in fruit and vegetables, and relatively low in fat and sugary foods. They should also have a diet that is low in salt and should not drink any alcohol until they are at least 16.

Adults and children should also drink plenty of fluids to keep them hydrated. Foods such as fruit, vegetables, soups, and stews are also a good source of fluid. Caffeinated drinks can make you dehydrated but decaffeinated ones can count as part of your fluid intake. A balanced diet is shown in the "healthy plate" below.

A balanced diet: the healthy plate (© Adam Merrin)

Children's diets across the years will now be described in detail.

Babies 0–6 months

Current recommendations state clearly that breast milk is the best possible food for all babies up until 6 months old. It contains the perfect nutritional mix for growth and development and also enables antibodies to be passed from the mother to the baby to help their immune system and defend against disease. There is also some evidence that breast milk helps expose the baby to a wide range of tastes as flavors from the mother's diet flow straight into the breast milk. Children like the foods they are familiar with (see Chapter 2). It is possible that early exposure through breast milk helps children to like a wider range of foods once they move on to solids.

When still in the womb the placenta acts as a filter and blocks some molecules from getting to the baby. Therefore, if you drink alcohol when pregnant, only some but not all of this alcohol will reach the fetus. Breasts do not have this filter so any alcohol you drink will go straight into the breast milk. For this reason it is recommended not to drink alcohol either while pregnant or while breast-feeding. The evidence for this remains weak, but to me personally, it seems to make sense. You wouldn't put alcohol in your baby's bottle so why put it in their breast milk?

While breast-feeding, the mother needs to eat a healthy balanced diet high in fruit and vegetables and brown bread, brown pasta, and brown rice and relatively low in fat and sugary foods. At this time mothers shouldn't try to eat for two or lose weight by eating a restricted diet. They should just eat a healthy diet to keep themselves and the baby well nourished.

But some women genuinely struggle to breast-feed and then feel guilty. Being a mum is a huge responsibility in so many ways, with so many possibilities for guilt and beating ourselves up. Therefore if you have weighed up the pros and cons and decide to stop breast-feeding, don't feel guilty. Just move on. And one benefit of not breast-feeding is that dads can take on a greater role in parenting, which may well keep them more involved in the longer term.

Babies 6–12 months

Current recommendations state that babies should be fully breast-fed (or bottle-fed) until 6 months when weaning onto solids can start. At first most of their food will still come from milk so the main aim of early weaning is to get them used to eating and encouraging them to try different tastes. Some mums make up ice-cube trays of mashed-up sweet potatoes or vegetables, or purée parts of their own meal to spoon-feed to their baby. Others hit the shelves of jars in the shops, while others toss their baby bits of finger food from their own plate to chew on. Nutritionally, at this stage it is probably best to create perfectly balanced frozen cubes of food which can be defrosted on time to be wolfed down by your compliant child. But life isn't always like that and the last thing you need at this stage is a parent frazzled by the food processor and cross with a baby who throws the carefully prepared food onto the floor. So psychologically (for you and your child) it is probably best to give your child a mix of a variety of foods including mashed-up vegetables, handy jars, and whatever you have on your plate, in order to keep your sanity and not make food into an issue.

Toddlers 12–24 months

As babies turn into toddlers they suddenly become much more active and their need for energy increases dramatically. At this age children move away from mashed-up food and start eating more adult-like meals. Children need energy, but they don't need sugar for energy, as although this might give them an immediate boost, their energy levels will quickly plummet, making them more tired than they were in the first place. So during this time they need a diet high in complex carbohydrates such as brown bread, brown pasta, and brown rice, high in fruit and vegetables, with moderate amounts of meat and fish, and relatively low in fat and sugary foods. They also need lots of dairy products for their calcium levels. But try to do the following:

- Keep the variety going.
- Give them plenty of savory foods.
- Eat with them when you can.
- Get them to eat with other children.
- Have regular meal times.

We like what we know (see Chapter 2) and now is the time to get them to know the tastes of the foods you will want them to like later on. It is also the time to start planting the seed of family eating, social eating, and planned eating, all of which are predictive of a healthy attitude as they grow up.

Children 2–5 years

By this stage most children should be eating a balanced diet high in complex carbohydrates and fruit and vegetables with a moderate amount of protein and low in fat and sugary foods. They shouldn't be on a low-fat diet as such and should now be drinking full fat milk and plenty of cheese for their fat and calcium intake. But neither should they be eating lots of high-fat foods such as crisps and deep fried chips. Children at this stage can become quite picky (called neophobia) and often refuse new foods, preferring to eat the same old familiar foods over and over again. Tips for overcoming this are described in Chapter 10, but simple approaches involve sheer persistence (putting it on their plate but not making a fuss about it), getting them to eat with other children, and eating different foods yourself in front of them. Some children seem to go through a stage when they hardly eat anything and live off air, while others seem forever hungry. Tips for managing children who either overeat or undereat are described in Chapters 12 and 13. But often these are just stages that they grow out of and the best way to help them to grow out of it is to ignore it. Making it into the focus of the dinner table can often make it worse.

Children 5–12

By age 5, recommendations suggest that children should eat the same kind of diet as adults. Ideally they also should be eating at the table, with the family, at regular meal times and eating the same food as everyone else. Obviously this is not always possible due to life getting in the way, but wherever possible try to include your children in with what and when you are eating. Also, have other children round for tea and send your child round to others for tea, to get them used to eating with others and as a means to get the healthy habits of their friends to rub off on them. Social eating and peer pressure are central to the way in which we decide which foods we like (see Chapter 2) and at this age this can be a useful strategy to encourage your own children to eat a more varied diet. Remember at this age you are still mostly in control of what they eat and most of their eating is done at home.

As for the school dinners versus packed lunch debate, I think there are pros and cons of both. You can control a packed lunch and fill it with healthy foods, but they can be very repetitive and children can get stuck in a rut of eating the same thing every day (and you have to buy it and prepare it every morning). School dinners may not always be the healthiest but they are bought and prepared by someone else and varied, and they encourage children to eat what they are given rather than what they have specifically requested the night before. But the choice is yours!

Teenagers 13–18

Children grow hugely in their teens and are bombarded by hormones that can make them starving all the time. It is also the time when they start to eat away from home more, have money to buy snacks, and become more influenced by their friends than by their parents. Nutritionally they need a healthy balanced diet the same as adults. But you might find that they need more snacks between meals, so make sure you have plenty of fruit, toast, cheese, crackers, yoghurt, breadsticks, and biscuits to keep them going.

So even if you can't control what they eat outside of the home, still provide healthy meals for when they are around, still have set meal times when they have to be back, and try to eat with them at the table as often as possible. Issues with body size might start to surface at this stage and tips for managing a child who feels fat are given in Chapter 14. Chapter 11 also deals with how to get your child to be more active, and Chapters 12 and 13 address overeating and undereating. But the most important factors are being a good role model yourself in terms of what you eat and how you talk about your body size and food, eating as a family, having regular meal times, and making chat, not food, the focus of the table.

Current recommendations for healthy eating in adults therefore describe a balanced and varied diet which is high in fruit and vegetables and complex carbohydrates and low in fat and sugary foods. Children's diets should approximate this, but can be higher in fat and dairy products until the age of 5. Children's diets should also be low in salt.

Why Eat a Healthy Diet?

Healthy eating is important for children as it impacts on health in two key ways: first, eating healthily in childhood helps growth and general development. Second, how we eat in childhood relates to how we eat as an adult and can either protect from or promote illnesses later in life. This chapter will now describe eating to be a healthy child and eating for a healthy life.

We are what we eat: start off as you mean to go on

Eating to be a healthy child

Children need a healthy diet to help them develop, grow, think, and learn. Every organ that they develop, every muscle they build, and every bone they make comes from the food they eat. So, although we don't understand the exact details of how each cell of our body is produced, it makes sense to give children a varied and balanced diet in order to increase the chances that it contains what they need to grow from tiny babies into fully grown adults.

Recently there has been much emphasis on obesity and the problem of being overweight. But this is only a tiny part of the problem. Regardless of body weight or how fat a child is, they need healthy food to grow strong teeth and bones, to develop a heart that works properly, a digestive system than can do its job, a set of lungs to breathe, and a brain that can keep them alive. And this all comes from food. I remember once reading about how many of the soldiers who died in the Vietnam War had heart disease, even at the age of 20, due to their diet. So even though these men looked at the peak of fitness in terms of their body size and shape, inside they were already diseased. And if children don't have a healthy diet, some may start to feel tired and breathless, suffer from asthma or joint problems, or be unable to keep up with their peers. But most will seem fine. Yet inside they may well be storing up problems for adulthood, as many of the problems adults face have started way before they are detected by the person themselves, let alone the health professionals they come into contact with.

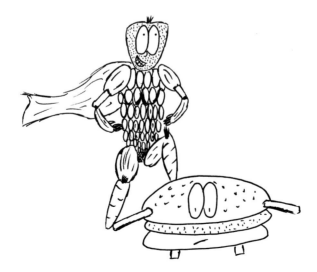

We are what we eat (© Adam Merrin)

Eating for a healthy life

Understanding children's diets is important not only in terms of the health of the child but also in terms of health later on in life, as there is some evidence that dietary habits acquired in childhood carry on into adulthood. For example, studies show that adults prefer to eat foods that they ate as children. In addition, long-term studies such as the Minnesota Heart Study and the Bogalusa Heart Study indicate that those who choose unhealthy foods as children continue to do so when they are grown up (3, 4). There is also some evidence for the impact of childhood nutrition on adult health. For example, poor fetal and infant growth seems to be linked with problems of managing blood sugar levels at age 64, and the levels of fat in the blood of the child have been shown to relate to adult heart disease. David Barker has specifically examined the role of both childhood and *in utero* nutrition in the development of adult illnesses and has provided evidence for his "Fetal Origins Hypothesis." His research indicates that early nutrition starting in the womb may relate to illnesses such as hypertension, heart disease, stroke, and chronic bronchitis (5).

Eating and Illness

An individual's health is influenced by a multitude of factors including their genetic makeup, their behavior, and their environment. Diet plays a central role and can contribute directly towards health. It can also impact on health through an interaction with a genetic predisposition. The effects of overeating, undereating, obesity, and eating disorders on health are discussed in Chapters 5–8. The impact of the actual composition of a person's diet on coronary heart disease, cancer, diabetes, and gallstones is described here.

Diet and coronary heart disease

The term "coronary heart disease" refers to a disease of the heart involving coronary arteries which are not functioning properly. The most important forms are angina (chest pain), heart attack, and sudden cardiac death. All these forms of heart disease are caused by narrowing of the arteries due to fatty deposits which obstruct the flow of blood. This is called atherosclerosis. Angina is a powerful pain in the chest, which sometimes radiates down the left arm. It develops when blood flow to the coronary arteries is restricted to such an extent that the heart muscle is starved of oxygen. An acute heart attack occurs when blood flow is restricted below a threshold level and some heart tissue is destroyed. It also seems to happen when a blood clot has further restricted blood flow to the heart. Sudden cardiac death typically occurs in patients who have already suffered damage to the heart through previous heart attacks, although it can occur in patients who previously seemed to have healthy arteries.

How common is heart disease?   Coronary heart disease (CHD) is responsible for 43 percent of deaths in men across Europe and 54 percent of deaths in women. In the UK, in 2008 CHD was responsible for 35 percent of deaths in men and 34 percent of deaths in women. It is the main cause of premature death in the UK (i.e. under 75 years) and worldwide it is estimated that 17 million people die from CHD each year, with the highest death rates being in China, India, and Russia. Deaths from CHD have declined in recent years in North America and across Europe, mainly due to the decline in smoking and other lifestyle factors. The highest death rates from CHD are found in men and women in the manual classes, and men and women of Asian origin. In middle age, the death rate is up to five times higher for men than for women; this evens out, however, in old age when CHD is the leading cause of death for both men and women. In the UK about 150,000 people each year survive a heart attack, with women showing poorer recovery than men in terms of both mood and activity levels.

Although biological factors play a part in coronary heart disease, diet is probably the fundamental factor. This is clearly shown by incidence of the disease in immigrant groups. For example, death from heart disease is very rare in Japan, but Japanese people who move to the West quickly show the pattern of mortality of their new environment – probably because they change their behavior. Coronary heart disease usually involves three factors: (i) narrowing of the arteries (atherosclerosis); (ii) a blood clot (thrombosis) and the impact of this, which can be sudden death, heart attack, angina, or no symptoms; this depends on (iii) the state of the heart muscle. Each of these three factors is influenced by different components of the diet.

Narrowing of the arteries   The material that accumulates in the arteries causing them to get narrower is cholesterol ester. Cholesterol ester exists in the blood and is higher in individuals with a genetic condition called familial hypercholesterolemia. Half of the cholesterol in the blood is created by the liver and half comes from the diet. Diet influences blood levels of cholesterol in two ways. First, blood cholesterol can be raised by saturated fat found in animal fat and in boiled, plunged, or espresso coffee (not instant or filtered). Second, blood cholesterol levels can be reduced by polyunsaturated fats found in plant oils, by soluble types of fiber such as pectin found in fruit and vegetables, by oat fiber found in vegetables, oatmeal, and oat bran, and by soya protein.

A blood clot (thrombosis)   A blood clot is caused by an increase in the clotting factors in the blood including Factor VIII, fibrinogen, and platelets. Under normal healthy conditions a blood clot is essential to stop unwanted bleeding. If there is already a degree of narrowing of the arteries this can cause a heart attack. The formation of blood clots is influenced by diet in the following ways: a fatty meal can increase Factor VIII; smoking and obesity are associated with increased fibrinogen; alcohol is associated with decreased fibrinogen; and fish oil (found in sardines, herring, mackerel, and salmon) has been shown to help prevent platelets from clustering together and causing a clot.

The state of the heart muscle   The general healthiness of the heart muscle may determine how an individual responds to having a thrombosis. An overall healthy diet consisting of a balance between the five food groups is associated with a healthier heart muscle.

Diet and blood pressure

Raised blood pressure (essential hypertension) is one of the main risk factors for coronary heart disease and is linked with heart attacks, angina, and strokes. It is more common in older people and is related to diet in the following ways.

Salt   Salt is the component of diet best known to affect blood pressure and can cause hypertension which is linked to heart disease, strokes, and kidney problems. As a means to reduce hypertension, it is recommended that we eat less than 6 g of salt per day, which is much less than that currently consumed by most people. Avoiding salt is difficult, however, as most of the salt consumed is not added at the table (9 percent) or added in cooking

(6 percent) but used in the processing of food (58.7 percent). For example, salted peanuts contain *less* salt than bread per 100 g. Many canned foods (such as baked beans) and breakfast cereals also have very high salt levels, which are masked by the sugar added.

Salt is also necessary, particularly in poorer countries where diarrhea is common, as it helps the body to rehydrate itself. In fact Britain imposed an extortionately high salt tax when it governed India, as salt was not only a useful flavor enhancer but also an essential part of the diet and therefore guaranteed a high level of revenue.

Alcohol   Alcohol consumption has several negative effects on health. For example, alcoholism increases the chances of liver cirrhosis, cancers (e.g. pancreas and liver), memory problems, and self-harm through accidents. Alcohol also increases the chances of hypertension; heavy drinkers have higher blood pressure than light drinkers and abstainers, and this has been shown to fall dramatically if alcoholic beer is replaced by low-alcohol beer.

In terms of alcohol's impact on mortality, data from the UK show that the number of deaths has more than doubled from 4,144 in 1991 to 8,380 in 2004. Data also show that death rates are higher for men than for women and that this gap has widened over recent years.

Alcohol may, however, also have a positive effect on health and there is some evidence that a glass of red wine per day may protect against heart disease. But, it is just as beneficial to drink cranberry juice, and much of the benefit from that one glass of wine is probably as much to do with stress reduction and the feeling of having a treat at the end of the day as the content of the wine itself.

Micronutrients   Several components of the diet have been hypothesized to lower blood pressure but evidence is still in the preliminary stages. For example, potassium found in foods such as potatoes, pulses, and dried fruits, calcium found in hard water, long-chain fatty acids found in fish oils, and magnesium found in foods such as bran, wholegrain cereals, and vegetables have been shown to reduce blood pressure.

Diet and cancer

Cancer is defined as an uncontrolled growth of abnormal cells, which produces tumors. There are two types of tumor: *benign* tumors, which do not spread throughout the body, and *malignant* tumors, which spread and create new tumors elsewhere (a process known as metastasis).

How common is cancer?   In 2008, cancer accounted for 7.6 million deaths worldwide (around 13 percent of all deaths) and it is now the leading cause of death. The main types of cancer are lung (1.4 million deaths), stomach (740,000 deaths), liver (700,000 deaths), colorectal (610,000 deaths), and breast (460,000 deaths). Deaths from cancer worldwide are predicted to continue to rise to over 11 million in 2030. The main causes of cancer mortality in the UK in 2008 were lung cancer (men: 7 percent; women: 5 percent), colorectal cancer (men and women: 3 percent), and breast cancer in women (4 percent). The incidence of newly diagnosed cancer in the UK in 2007 indicates that the most commonly diagnosed cancers in men are prostate cancer (24 percent) and lung cancer (22 percent) and in women breast cancer (31 percent) and colorectal cancer (12 percent).

  Diet is believed to account for more variation in the incidence of all cancers than any other factor, even smoking. But how diet affects cancer is unclear. One theory is that all foodstuffs contain natural non-nutrients which can trigger cancer. Such factors have been shown to cause mutations in the laboratory, but there is no evidence that they can do the same in human beings. A second theory claims that a poor diet weakens the body's defense mechanisms. The cancers most clearly related to diet are those of the esophagus, stomach, and large intestine. There is also a possible link with breast cancer.

Esophageal cancer   The rates of esophageal cancer vary enormously around the world and are at their highest in China, Iran, and South Africa. The strongest dietary factor in the development of esophageal cancer is alcohol, particularly when the alcohol is derived from apples, and this often works in association with the impact of smoking. Other dietary factors which have been hypothesized to be associated with esophageal cancer include vitamin deficiencies and moldy food.

Stomach cancer   The incidence of stomach cancer has halved in the past 25 years in Britain but is at its highest in Japan. Data suggest that salt and pickled and salted foods trigger stomach cancer, while fruit and vegetables, the refrigeration of foods, and vitamin C intake are protective.

Bowel cancer   Cancer of the bowel is the second largest cause of death from cancer in Britain and is 10 times more common in Britain and the US than in developing countries. Rates in Scotland have been among the highest in the world. Evidence suggests that wheat fiber and vegetables may be protective, while animal fat and meat (particularly if well cooked) and some types of beer may trigger bowel cancer.

Breast cancer   Breast cancer is the largest cause of death from cancer in women in Britain, with the majority of cases occurring in women who are post-menopausal. Possible dietary links with breast cancer include high fat intake and weight gain as predictive, and wheat fiber and soya as protective.

Diet and diabetes mellitus

There are two types of diabetes. Type 1 diabetes always requires insulin and is also called childhood onset diabetes. Some evidence has pointed towards a role for genetic factors, and research has also indicated that it is more common in those children who were not exclusively breast-fed for the first three to four months of life. Type 2 diabetes tends to develop later on in life and can be managed by diet alone. This form of diabetes shows a clearer relationship with diet. Type 2 diabetes seems to be mainly a complication of being overweight, and the risk of developing it is greater in those who show weight around the middle rather than on the thighs or buttocks. It is generally assumed that Type 2 diabetes is associated with diets high in sugar as people with diabetes struggle to manage their blood sugar levels. Evidence for this association is poor, and high fat intake seems to be its main dietary predictor, with high fiber and high carbohydrate intakes being protective.

Diet and gallstones and urinary tract stones

Gallstones are more likely to occur in women and certain ethnic groups. Obesity and dieting with rapid weight loss can increase the risk of gallstones, while moderate alcohol intake and vegetarian and high fiber diets are protective. Urinary tract stones can be made of either calcium or oxalate. Calcium stones are related to diets rich in protein, sodium, sugar, vitamin D, calcium, alcohol, curry, and spicy foods and low in cereal fiber and water. Oxalate stones are related to diets rich in foods containing oxalates such as spinach, rhubarb, beetroot, and tea, and diets low in water.

Who Has a Healthy Diet?

We therefore know that we should feed our children a diet high in fruit and vegetables and complex carbohydrates and relatively low in fat and sugary foods. We also know that diet is linked to a number of illnesses such as coronary heart disease, cancer, diabetes, and gallstones. So how many people actually eat a healthy diet?

Children's diets

Many children's diets in the Western world are unsatisfactory. For example, a large study in the US showed that the majority of 10-year-olds have diets too high in total fat, saturated fat, and dietary cholesterol. Similarly, surveys in the UK show that 75 percent of children aged 10 to 11 consume more than the recommended level of fat and that the majority of 9–11-year-old British children consume less than half the recommended daily intake of fruit and vegetables, with only 5 percent of children eating more (6, 7). Research also shows that while children's diets tend to be acceptable for protein levels they are often too high in sugar (mostly from fizzy drinks), too high in salt, and lacking in vitamin A, vitamin D, and iron (causing high levels of anemia). Further, about 20 percent of this excess fat intake comes from snacks.

Malnutrition in children   Dietary recommendations aimed at Western countries in the main emphasize a reduction in food intake and the avoidance of overweight. Undereating and malnutrition are the key problem for the developing world, however, resulting in both physical and psychological problems and poor resistance to illness. Recent data from the World Health Organization (WHO) concluded that 174 million children under the age of 5 in the developing world were underweight for their age, with 230 million being stunted in their growth. Further, WHO estimates that 54 percent of childhood mortality is caused by malnutrition, particularly related to a deficit of protein and energy consumption. Such malnutrition is highest in South Asia, where it is estimated to be five times higher than in the Western hemisphere, followed by Africa, then Latin America.

One common problem is the low energy content of the foods used to wean children which can lead to growth problems and ultimate malnutrition. In particular, breast milk is an essential source of fat for children, and is often the main source of fat until the child is 2 years old. Problems occur, however, when children are weaned onto low-fat adult food. These lowered energy diets can sustain health in the absence of illness, but are insufficient to provide "catch up" growth if the child is ill with infections such as diarrhea. WHO states that malnutrition occurs in virtually all countries, as even when the majority of a country's population has access to sufficient food a minority can still be deprived.

Eating in young adults

Many eating habits are established in childhood. They are then further crystallized in the first years of independence when individuals become responsible for their own food choices and food preparation. Research has therefore explored the diets of young adults. One large-scale study at the beginning of the 1990s examined the eating behavior of 16,000 male and female students aged between 18 and 24 from 21 European countries (8). Overall, the results showed that 39 percent tried to avoid fat, 41 percent tried to eat fiber, 53.5 percent ate fruit daily, 54 percent limited their consumption of red meat, and 68 percent limited salt. These results suggest that the prevalence of these fairly basic healthy eating practices was low in this large sample of young adults. In terms of gender differences the results showed that women were more likely to try to avoid fat and cholesterol, to eat more fiber, to avoid red meat, and to eat fruit daily; men and women were similar in their use of salt. Women across Europe therefore seemed to have healthier diets than men.

In 2001 a similar large-scale survey was carried out to assess the diets of young people aged 19 and 24 years in the UK (9). The results from this survey indicated that 98 percent consumed fewer than the five portions of fruit and vegetables recommended per day (average 1.6 portions). They consumed more saturated fat than is recommended and more sugar, mostly from fizzy drinks, consumption of which had increased from 3–4 cans per week in 1986/1987 to 8–9 cans per week in 2000/2001. Their diets were also deficient in vitamin D, vitamin A, and iron (again particularly those of women). Therefore young people's diets are not matching the

---

Take home points

- For adults, a healthy diet is: lots of fruit and vegetables, lots of brown bread, brown rice, and brown pasta, some meat and fish and dairy products, not many sweets or foods high in fat (i.e. fried foods). Adults should also cut down on alcohol and salt.
- For children, a healthy diet is: lots of fruit and vegetables, lots of brown bread, brown rice, and brown pasta, some meat and fish, not many sweets or fried foods. Children should eat more dairy products than adults and can eat more fat. Children should also have a diet low in salt and no alcohol.
- Children need a varied diet.
- Children will eventually eat what their parents eat, so be a good role model.
- Don't make food into a battle for children – it will backfire on you as they get older.

---

recommended intakes and are particularly high in saturated fat and sugar and low in fruit and vegetables.

Adult diets

Unfortunately, poor diets are also common in adulthood. One large-scale survey in 2001 in the UK (9) reported that although 86 percent of adults surveyed ate less than the five recommended portions of fruit and vegetables per day (average 2.8 per day), intake had increased by 0.4 portions per day since the previous survey in 1986/1987. Adult diets were also found to be too high in sugar, salt, and alcohol and deficient in iron and vitamin D. Compared to 10 years previously, the intake of red meat, meat-based dishes, and processed meat and saturated fat had decreased.

In Summary

Children should eat a diet high in complex carbohydrates such as brown bread, brown pasta, and brown rice and high in fruit and vegetables. After the age of 5, their diets should be relatively low in fat and sugary foods such as sweets, cakes, and biscuits, which should only make up a small part of what they eat. In addition, their salt intake should be low and they shouldn't drink any alcohol. Children's diets are important as not only does a healthy diet help them grow and develop, but what they learn to eat in childhood will have a huge influence on what they eat once they are adults. Furthermore, once they are adults their diet may cause, or protect them from, a wide range of illnesses such as coronary heart disease, cancer, diabetes, and gallstones. Yet we know that the diets of children and young adults are often poor and particularly low in fruit and vegetables and high in fat and salt.

2

How do we learn to like the food we like?

When asked why and when they eat or don't eat, most people say "I like it," "it tastes nice," or "I was hungry," which is in line with a more biological model of eating behavior and the biological sensations of hunger and fullness. But people eat differently according to their culture, ethnicity, and family history. When they move from one country to another their diets and food preferences change, and when people share their lives with others from different backgrounds they adjust their food choices accordingly. Given the enormous cultural diversity in food preferences it is generally accepted that food choice is more complex than simply a matter of biological drives. Psychological models of eating have therefore been developed which focus on how we learn to like the foods we like from the moment we are born (and possibly even before), and how our preferences are shaped by the people around us. When we feed our children, we are therefore not only shaping the foods they will eat and like as children, but we are also shaping when, why, and what they will eat for the rest of their lives. This chapter will therefore explore why we eat what we eat in terms of the following:

Biological models:
- Taste, hunger, and fullness

Psychological models:
- Exposure
- Role models
- Learning by association
- Parental control

The Good Parenting Food Guide: Managing What Children Eat without Making Food a Problem, First Edition. Jane Ogden.
© 2014 John Wiley & Sons, Ltd. Published 2014 by John Wiley & Sons, Ltd.

Good parenting . . .

Eating is about so much more than taste, hunger, and fullness. We eat what we like and we like what we have learned to like through familiarity, watching others, and associations with our mood and the people around us. Good parenting is about helping our children to learn to like a healthy diet and to establish eating habits that can carry them through the rest of their lives.

Biological Models of Eating Behavior

Eating is a basic biological requirement and without food and drink we would die. It has been around forever and should have evolved in ways that can keep us healthy and alive. We therefore tend to believe that we have innate preferences for foods and that we like certain foods because our ancestors did. To test this theory, newborn babies have been given differently flavored milk and their preference has been assessed using facial expressions and the speed of their sucking behavior. The results show that newborn babies innately prefer sweet and salty tastes and reject bitter tastes (10).

Evolutionarily speaking, it is believed that a preference for sweet foods comes from the need to consume berries and fruits, that the preference for salty foods reflects the need for fish and meat, and that the dislike of bitter tastes protects us against poisonous foods and those which have gone moldy. This is the evidence for innate preferences. *But*, those babies who were given sweetened milk in the first week of the above study showed an even greater preference for more sweetened milk the week after, indicating that even at such a young age babies are learning what to like based upon what they are being given; the sweeter the milk they are familiar with, the sweeter they like it. It seems that even the apparently innate preference for sweet tastes can be modified by familiarity.

Furthermore, we may have an innate preference for sugar, evolutionarily speaking, but we do not eat actual sugar. We eat the cultural version of sugar called "biscuits," "cake," "baklava," "kulfi," or "wagashi," depending upon what we are used to. We may also have a biological aversion to bitter

tastes, but coffee, which epitomizes bitterness, is the most frequently consumed "drug" worldwide and is drunk by the bucketful even when decaffeinated. And similarly we know that although some cultures, such as the
Japanese, consume high levels of salt, when people from these cultures
move countries they quickly change their taste preferences to be in line
with their new environment. Therefore, what foods we like may have some
biological basis but it is easily and quickly modified by learning and by our
environment.

A similar picture arises for feelings of hunger and fullness. Ask yourself
the following questions:

- Do you eat when you are hungry?
- Do you eat when you are bored?
- Do you eat when you are fed up?
- Do you eat more when you go out for dinner for a friend's birthday than
  you would at home?
- Do you eat more on a Sunday lunchtime at home compared to a
  Tuesday lunchtime at work, even though it's the same time on both
  days?
- When you go out for dinner do you ever ask "who's for pudding?"
  because it's embarrassing to eat chocolate profiteroles alone with every-
  one watching?
- And, do you only ever eat when you are hungry?

I have asked these questions in many talks over the years and although I
have the occasional person who eats only for hunger, pretty much everyone
else eats according to their emotions, whether they are alone or with others
or whether the meal is a special occasion or just a routine part of the day.
Food is about so much more than just staying alive. For this reason, I
believe that the best answer to the question "why do we like the foods we
like" emphasizes learning and psychology.

Psychological Models of Eating Behavior

Children in the UK like pizza, chicken nuggets, chips, and baked beans.
But children in Japan eat fish, those in China eat noodles, those in India
eat spiced curry, those in Greece eat salad, and those in Libya eat couscous.
Do these children have different taste-buds or are they just reacting to their

culture and what they are being given? Similarly, while breakfasts in the UK mostly consist of cereal or toast, Germans eat ham and cheese, Italians drink black coffee and have a pastry, and people in China eat rice. And have you ever thought "I eat everything," then lived with a partner who likes chips more than you? Hates sauces when you don't? Doesn't like "mixed up food"? Or likes to have meat with every meal when you would prefer not to? Food preferences vary hugely between cultures. But even within cultures, different families have their own habits, likes, and dislikes which can suddenly highlight how you too have a specific way of liking your food to be.

All these differences illustrate a strong role for psychological factors. In particular, they illustrate the impact of four key factors: exposure, learning from role models, learning by association, and parental control.

Exposure

The theory of exposure simply describes the impact of familiarity on food preferences. Human beings need to consume a variety of foods in order to have a balanced diet and yet show fear and avoidance of new foods (called neophobia). Young children will therefore show neophobic responses to a new food but must come to accept and eat foods which may originally appear to be threatening. In line with this, studies show that simply exposing children to foods over and over again can change children's preferences. In fact several studies indicate that the magic number is about 10 times. But I know it took my children about 327 times to give in to eating broccoli, so the rule is to just keep going.

So children in the UK like pizza, Chinese children like rice, and Japanese children like fish *not* because their taste-buds are different but because this is the food they are familiar with. And if a British child were transported to Japan, very soon they would like Japanese food and vice versa. If we want our child to like different food we simply have to keep giving it to them.

Learning from role models

Modeling describes the impact of watching other people's behavior on our own behavior and is sometimes referred to as "social learning" or "observational learning." Early research focused on aggression and showed that children became more aggressive if they had watched an adult being aggressive. In terms of eating, we learn what foods we like from a number of role models including peers, parents, and the media.

Peers   An early study explored the impact of "social suggestion" on children's eating behaviors, and arranged to have children observe a series of role models eating foods that were different from what they were used to. The role models chosen were other children, an unknown adult, and a fictional hero. The results showed a greater change in the child's food preference if the model was an older child, a friend, or the fictional hero. The unknown adult had no impact on food preferences (11).

In one study, children who liked peas (but not carrots) were seated next to children who liked carrots (but not peas) at lunch for a week. By the end of the study the children had changed their vegetable preference and were eating both peas and carrots. They were still eating both several weeks later when the children were followed up (12). Therefore, simply watching other children changed the foods that children liked and ate.

In another study, children with a history of being picky eaters watched a video showing older children called "food dudes" enthusiastically eating a wide range of foods and making comments such as "these beans are so crunchy." The results showed that after exposure to the "food dudes" the picky eaters changed their food preferences and started to eat fruit and vegetables (13).

Food preferences therefore change through watching others eat.

Parents   Parental attitudes to food and eating behaviors are also central to the process of modeling. For example, we know that parents and their children of all ages tend to like and eat the same foods. We also know that even when children leave home they tend to eat the diet they developed while at home, which is similar to that of their parents in terms of snacking, what they eat at meal times, and even how much they eat. In fact, even if children break away from their parents' diets in their teenage years they tend to return to them after their rebellious period is over and they start to settle down. So parents are an important source of learning, and often the best way to change a child's diet is to change the parents' diet first.

We learn to like food by watching others (© Adam Merrin)

The media   Television, magazines, the internet, and films are an ever increasing source of role models for children, and although cigarette and alcohol advertising has been banned in most Western countries, food advertising has not. In fact unhealthy foods are given almost twice as much airtime as healthy foods during TV aimed at the under-fives. The role of modeling by the media can be shown by three "big events" over the past few decades.

Audrey Eyton's F-Plan Diet: This was published in 1982 and received a great deal of media attention. It recommended a high fiber diet and within a week sales of bran-based cereals rose by 30 percent, wholewheat bread sales rose by 10 percent, wholewheat pasta by 70 percent, and baked beans by 8 percent.

Edwina Currie and the egg scare: In December 1988 the then junior health minister in the UK said on television that "most of the egg production in this country, sadly, is now infected with salmonella." Pretty much overnight, egg sales fell by 50 percent, and by the end of 1989 sales were still only at 75 percent of their previous levels.

Mad cow disease: Between May and August in 1990 there was massive publicity about the health risks of eating beef due to "mad cow disease." This resulted in a 20 percent reduction in beef sales in the UK.

These large-scale one-off media scares dramatically changed how people ate. Imagine what ongoing advertising every day in between TV programs, flashing up on computers, or on the glossy pages of magazines can do to the foods we feel like eating. In fact several studies show that if children are shown adverts for both healthy and unhealthy foods in a laboratory, not only are they more likely to remember the adverts for unhealthy foods but they also eat more unhealthy foods later on.

We therefore learn what foods we like from our peers, our parents, and the media. These are our key role models and they help form which foods we like and which foods we actually eat.

Learning by association

The third psychological mechanism that influences how we learn to like foods is learning through association. The classic early study was by Ivan Pavlov who showed that if he rang a bell each time he gave his dog some food, after a while the dog started to salivate when the bell was rung, even if the food wasn't there. Pavlov argued that the dog had learned to associate the bell with food and therefore reacted in the same way to the bell as he reacted to food. This is known as "conditioning." Similarly, B.F. Skinner showed that if he rewarded pigeons for pressing a lever with food then they learned to press the lever more often. This is known as "reinforcement." In terms of eating behavior there is a wealth of research showing that both conditioning and reinforcement help us learn which foods we like; we like foods if we associate them with positive feelings or situations *and* if we are positively reinforced for eating them. There are three ways in which learning changes what we like to eat.

Rewarding healthy eating   If you say to a child *"if you eat your vegetables I will be pleased with you"* and then smile and praise them when they do, after a while they will start to actually prefer these foods. The foods become associated with praise; praise is nice so the foods become nice. Rewarding eating behavior seems to improve food preferences. Similarly, if you give your child broccoli, and pull a face, saying "Try it, but you might not like it, it's a strange taste," they will associate broccoli with something unpleasant and won't grow to like it.

Using food as a reward for good behavior   If you say to a child *"if you are well behaved you can have a biscuit"* you are using food as a reward to change a child's behavior. This has positive effects on their behavior in the short term and makes it more likely that they will do their homework, go to bed on time, or tidy their room. *But*, in the longer term, studies show that using food as a reward makes them see the biscuit as special and a treat and therefore makes them like it even more. So using food as a reward is a useful short-term trick to get children to behave as we want them to, but in the longer term it promotes a preference for unhealthy "treat" foods. *Then* in the future when they are feeling fed up, bored, or lonely these treat foods are the perfect solution as this is what they have been taught as a child.

We learn which foods are treats (© Creativa / Shutterstock)

Using food as a reward for healthy eating   Many parents say *"if you eat your vegetables you can eat your pudding"* and use unhealthy food as a reward for eating healthy food. This, again, may work in the short term as children will eat their vegetables. But in the longer term they are learning that pudding is a treat and that vegetables are not nice as "my mum has to bribe me to eat them." In an early study researchers told children stories about imaginary foods called "hupe" and "hule" and said "There were two foods on the table but Jenny could only eat the 'hupe' if she had eaten the 'hule.'" The children listening were then asked which one they would like to eat the most, and they all wanted the "hupe" – the reward one (14). So rewarding food with food may work in the short term but in the longer term it teaches the child to prefer the treat food as this is being framed as special and something that needs to be earned.

We therefore learn to like the foods we like through learning by association and reinforcement. If we reward healthy eating through smiling and praise then this seems to work and can help children to prefer a healthier diet. But if we use unhealthy foods to reward either good behavior or healthy eating, then, although this may be a useful quick fix, in the longer term children will learn to prefer the foods that have been offered as treats and avoid those foods that we really want them to eat.

Parental control

The next factor which seems to impact upon how children learn to like certain foods is the role of parental control. We currently live in a world where crisp bags are getting bigger, burgers and chips are offered as a mid-afternoon snack, and sweets and chocolate are sold at child height just when you are frantically sorting out your shopping trolley and resistance is low. Many parents therefore impose some form of control over what their child eats.

This can involve trying to get your child to eat less by saying:

"That's enough Easter egg now. Save the rest for tomorrow."
"No you can't have pudding. Not until you have eaten your meal."
"Please don't have any more biscuits, I'm cooking dinner."
"Please wait now and have a biscuit after dinner."
"Just have a small piece of cake now. Have some more tomorrow."
"Those are mum's biscuits. Not for you. You can't have any."

It may also involve trying to get them to eat more:

"Please clean your plate. Plenty of people would be glad of that food."
"Just have a few more vegetables before you get down."
"Just five more peas please then you can have some ice cream."
"How about another slice of cake?"
"Those chips are lovely. Do finish them off. I don't want them to go to waste."
"You look tired. Have a piece of chocolate to give you some energy."

And for some parents it involves watching and monitoring; standing behind their child at meal times or even next to them when they are eating with friends, making sure that they don't eat too much or too little.

Much research has explored the consequences of different types of parental control over children's diets, and the findings suggest that it is all quite complicated. Ideally we wouldn't need to control what our children eat and could let them make their own choices and rely upon some natural process of healthy food selection. But in a world full of crisps, chocolate, and burgers and chips, some form of control seems necessary. Therefore, in general I think that there are helpful and unhelpful ways to control what your child eats (see Table 2.1).

Helpful control The goal of helpful control is to have some say in what your child eats, so that you can encourage them to have a healthy diet, without making them preoccupied with the very foods you want them to avoid, *and* without giving them something to rebel against later on. If you make healthy eating into an obsession, once they hit their teens and really want to annoy you, they will use food as the perfect tool. But if you introduce healthy eating without them realizing it, you give them nothing to rebel against when the time comes. Helpful control comes in the form of what you do and what you say:

Manage their environment: By far the best way to control what a child eats is to manage their environment without them even knowing it. So don't bring foods into the house that you don't want them to eat, take them to healthy cafés and restaurants, and cook them food that is good for them. This way you can have some say in what they eat but you won't make them preoccupied with what they can't eat.

Be a good role model: Be seen to eat the foods you want them to eat. This way they won't realize you are controlling them and they will have nothing to rebel against later on.

Speak positively about healthy food: When you are around healthy food speak about it in ways that make your child think they are nice. Say "this shepherd's pie is great," "this cauliflower is really crunchy," or "these carrots are so sweet." And soon they will learn to eat what you are eating without any idea that they are learning these things because you want them to.

Praise them for eating well: Praise in the form of words and smiles can change what they eat, so when they try broccoli and say they don't like it, say "well done for trying. It was quite nice really!" When they eat all their sausages and mash, say "well done – you did enjoy that!" And when they say they can't eat any more as they are full, say "that's fine. It's good to know when you have had enough."

Table 2.1   What parents say changes how children think about food

Things to say	Try not to say
This shepherd's pie is great!	I know broccoli isn't very nice but it's good for you.
This cucumber is really juicy!	Have something healthy for a change.
These carrots are so sweet!	After tea we can have something nice.
Well done for trying. It was quite nice really!	Those are mum's biscuits. Not for you. You can't have any.
Well done – you did enjoy that!	You do have a huge appetite.
You are so good at trying new foods.	You are a bottomless pit!
You are good at knowing when to stop eating.	She does really like her pudding!
It's good to know when you have had enough.	He has a really sweet tooth!
Just eat a bit more.	Just have a small piece of cake now. Have some more tomorrow.
She's so good at eating vegetables.	That's enough Easter egg now. Save the rest for later.
Stay at the table a bit longer.	No you can't have pudding. Not until you have eaten your meal.
Just a few more vegetables.	Just five more peas please then you can have some ice cream.
Please don't have any more biscuits, I'm cooking dinner. You can have them afterwards.	Eat your vegetables then you can have pudding.
We have a lovely melon for pudding.	You look tired. Have a piece of chocolate to give you some energy.
Please wait now and have a biscuit after dinner.	That took me ages to cook. Please eat it all.
If you are hungry have some fruit.	Eat that last biscuit for me will you.
Dinner is at 6. Just wait now.	
Here's some lovely carrot sticks to munch on before bed.	

Encourage them without pressure: Young children, in particular, get bored of sitting at the table and often want to get down after the first few mouthfuls. It is fine to say "just eat a bit more," or "stay at the table a bit longer," or "just a few more vegetables." But the line between encouragement and pressure is a thin one, so try to do this in a light-hearted manner and if they really don't want to eat any more then leave them alone.

Set a daily structure: We live in a world where we tend to have three meals spread across the day. Children therefore have to learn this pattern in order to fit in. This also means that they need to learn that feeling hungry before a meal is a good thing as food is on its way and the hungrier they are the more they will enjoy their meal. It is therefore fine to limit your child's snacking and say "Please don't have any more biscuits, I'm cooking dinner. You can have them afterwards."

Set a meal structure: We want children to eat more savory, unsweetened foods than puddings so they also need to learn that any puddings come after the main meal. This way they will use up their hunger on the healthy foods and feel less hungry by the time dessert arrives. It is therefore also fine to say "Please wait now and have a biscuit after dinner." *But*, don't make the biscuits the reward for eating dinner; they just come afterwards.

Helpful control that involves managing the environment, being a good role model, and saying the right things that encourage healthy eating without pressure or making sweets into a reward can be a useful way of trying to manage what children eat. These are also ways of imposing some element of control without doing harm, without making children preoccupied with the foods you don't want them to eat, and without giving them something to react against later on.

Unhelpful control   Most other forms of control can be unhelpful and may do harm. And although they might offer an immediate quick fix, in the longer term a child may well learn to prefer the foods you are trying to get them to avoid. In fact, many studies show that as they grow up, children tend to prefer the foods that have been banned and when their parents leave the room they reach straight for the foods that have usually been restricted. Unhelpful forms of control also take the form of what you do and what you say and can backfire as the child grows up. Here are different forms of unhelpful control and descriptions of what children are learning when they are used:

Overt restriction: If you bring unhealthy food into the house that you would rather your child didn't eat then you will need to control their behavior in ways that they will know about. This is known as "overt control" and might involve having a sweet cupboard that they can't reach, a chocolate drawer that is for "mummy and daddy" or "special occasions," or a huge cake that they can only have a small slice of. So try not to say "Those are mum's biscuits. Not for you. You can't have any," "Just have a small piece of cake now. Have some more tomorrow," or "That's enough Easter egg now. Save the rest for later." Imagine your partner buying you the perfect necklace (ring, boots, perfume, cake?), then placing it in a glass jar and not letting you have it. Pretty soon you would be cross and obsessing about it *and* sneaking down in the night to smash the jar into pieces! This may well be what some children feel like when they know you have bought something that they are simply not allowed, as they learn that these foods are special and forbidden, which is a toxic combination.

Rewarding food with food: As described under the section on learning by association, rewarding food with food can backfire in the longer term and is a form of control which doesn't really work. So try not to say "No you can't have pudding. Not until you have eaten your meal" or "Just five more peas please then you can have some ice cream" or "Eat your vegetables then you can have pudding." They might eat their meal and their five peas but they will have learned that pudding and ice cream are much nicer.

Pressure to eat between meals: When my children were little I observed many mums giving their children food even when their child didn't seem hungry. So they would say "How about another slice of cake?" even when the child hadn't asked for it, or "You look tired. Have a piece of chocolate to give you some energy." If children are pressured to eat even when they aren't hungry they struggle to learn what hunger feels like and then fail to learn that eating takes that hunger away. Children need to get hungry between meals so that they learn to manage this sensation and, as adults, know that this sensation means "get ready to eat soon" rather than "I am unhappy or bored or lonely." Anticipating your child's every need may feel like attentive parenting but it prevents a child from learning what their own needs are and how they can fulfill them on their own.

Pressure to eat at meals: I have also observed many mums hovering around their child at tea time spooning in extra food (way after the child could feed themselves) and going beyond the usual encouragement that

Take home points

- We are born with an innate liking of sweet and salty foods.
- *But* we start to learn what we like as soon as we are born.
- We like foods that we are familiar with.
- We learn what to like from parents, peers, and the media.
- We like food if we associate it with nice things (praise, a treat, a reward).
- Parents try to control their children's diets but not always in helpful ways.
- Helpful control includes managing their environment, being a good role model, and praising healthy eating.
- Unhelpful control includes pressure, rewarding food with food, and making food forbidden.

is sometimes necessary. I was brought up by parents who had experienced rationing and real hunger during wartime and was often told "Please clean your plate. Plenty of people would be glad of that food" or "If I could, I'd send that to the poor starving children in Africa." Wasted food was a real sin and we were encouraged to eat everything in front of us. Nowadays children are subjected to other forms of pressure such as "That took me ages to cook. Please eat it all" and "Do you know how much that cost?" None of these are very helpful approaches as the child learns to eat according to what is there rather than how hungry they are. And this again means that they don't learn to recognize the feeling of hunger and that eating will make it go away. Sometimes parents also get their children to eat the food they would like to eat themselves but can't because they are on a diet, saying "Those chips are lovely. Do finish them off" or "Eat that last biscuit for me will you." So the child eats when they don't want to and the parent uses them as a human dustbin!

There are therefore many forms of control which can be quite unhelpful. In particular, buying in food then obviously limiting it can make children rebel later on and become preoccupied with the very foods you are trying to limit. Similarly, rewarding food with food makes the reward food into even more of a treat, and pressuring children to eat when they are no longer hungry stops them from learning what hunger is and how eating can take it away.

In Summary

Although we may believe that we eat because we like it or when we are hungry, eating behavior and food preferences are much more complicated than some innate drive to keep us alive. Eating is a cultural and psychological behavior that is learned from the moment we are born and influenced by simple exposure and familiarity, learning from role models and by association and in response to the ways food is controlled by our parents. Strategies to manage your child's diet in a healthy way are considered in more detail in the tips and reality chapters in the second half of this book.

3

What does food mean to us and what role does it play in our lives?

For biologists, food means staying healthy and alive. In times of famine this is still very much the case and we are all familiar with images of hungry children and adults in countries torn apart by war, drought, floods, earthquakes, or storms. Even in developed countries, which seem relatively stable, levels of malnutrition are surprisingly high as parents struggle to feed their children a healthy diet, or those who are homeless live from hand to mouth. But fortunately, for the majority in the developed world, food is not such a luxury, and because of this our relationship with food has grown ever more wide-ranging and complex. As Todhunter said in 1973:

> food is prestige, status and wealth . . . an "apple for the teacher" or an expression of hospitality, friendship, affection, neighbourliness, comfort and sympathy in time of sadness or danger. It symbolises strength, athleticism, health and success. It is a means of pleasure and self gratification and a relief from stress. It is feasts, ceremonies, rituals, special days and nostalgia for home, family and the "good old days" . . . a means of self expression and a way of revolt. Most of all it is tradition, custom and security . . . There are Sunday foods and weekday foods, family foods and guest foods; foods with magical properties and health and disease foods. (15)

These many meanings influence the ways in which we eat and how we provide food for those around us. It is important to understand these many

The Good Parenting Food Guide: Managing What Children Eat without Making Food a Problem, First Edition. Jane Ogden.
© 2014 John Wiley & Sons, Ltd. Published 2014 by John Wiley & Sons, Ltd.

meanings of food as through our parenting during their childhood our children are learning what food means to them, which will influence what and why they eat for the rest of their lives.

This chapter will focus on the complex meanings of food in terms of:

- Emotional regulation
- Conflict
- Control
- Social interaction
- Identity and communication

To illustrate these meanings I will draw upon interviews I have conducted with a range of people, including those who are overweight or have been, those who have had an eating disorder, and those who are normal weight but who have spoken openly about their relationship with food.

Good parenting . . .

Food is no longer just about survival. In today's world food has many meanings relating to emotions, conflict, control, how we interact with others, and how we make statements about who we are. These meanings influence when, what, and how much we eat and, when things go wrong, may spiral into over- or undereating. Good parenting is about understanding these many meanings and helping our children to develop a healthy relationship with food which is as close to "easy", "neutral," and "nice" as possible. Food may be one of life's pleasures, but food as an obsession can lead to a life of worry and upset, and this needs to be avoided wherever possible.

Food and Emotional Regulation

In the 1970s researchers developed the emotionality theory of eating behavior and argued that people became obese or overweight because they ate for emotional reasons more than thinner people. The obese were therefore considered to eat when they were upset, bored, anxious, or for comfort, whereas the non-obese ate when they were hungry. Similarly, Hilda Bruch described how people with eating disorders used food to regulate their emotions and often ate because they interpreted the internal signals of emotional need as the need for food (16). Much recent research, however, indicates that most people eat for emotional reasons, not just the obese or those with eating disorders, and that for the majority, different foods are encoded with meanings such as comfort, pleasure, boredom, upset, and relief and are central to celebration and the need for indulgence. These meanings are learned from our childhood through the processes of reward and association and they provide us with a rich set of beliefs about food.

At times people eat to manage stress:

"We all have stresses and strains over the years of different things and bereavements that all contribute to why we eat more."

And similarly:

"I had a lot of family commitments at the time, there was a lot of problems with my husband and my daughter who didn't get on and I was depressed over it, you know, and I just felt that I was in the middle. And erm I think that was the main problem and we had money problems and what have you and my way of coping was eating."

Many people also eat when they are bored:

"I'd just eat, used to eat just, you know, not because I was hungry, just because I was bored or fed up or you know there was nothing else to do."

Some also eat when they are depressed:

"Food is . . . when you're depressed, it's your companion isn't it? You wanna have a good time you're gonna eat and you'll eat anything you know . . . I mean I don't go out, I don't drink, I don't smoke . . ."

And many people specifically describe their behavior as comfort eating:

"Now I could eat a bit of chocolate if I'm upset or I'm tired or feeling vulnerable, I will go for the chocolate or crisps so I can comfort eat . . . I think it's important to eat something but if it's chocolate or sweets it's better to comfort eat . . ."

Food is therefore used by many as a means to regulate their emotions. This process, however, is not always straightforward and often generates conflicts for the individual. As one woman said:

> "I use it so much to control my emotions although of course it never does and makes it worse. It's not a friend but it's an emotional support . . . I have a sort of love–hate relationship with food."

Food and Conflict

Food is therefore strongly linked with our emotional lives and can be used as a means of emotional regulation. This process, however, generates a range of conflicts as food is often associated with opposite sets of meanings, such as eating versus denial, guilt versus pleasure, and health versus pleasure.

Eating versus denial

Media images tell women, and increasingly men, that they should stay thin in order to be attractive, yet at the same time they need to provide food for their families if they are to be good wives and good mothers. This can create a conflict between eating and denial. Marilyn Lawrence, who is a therapist, described this conflict in her patients with eating disorders, saying "eating is a source of pleasure, but not often for the people who have the primary responsibility for providing it. Women take control of food, while simultaneously denying themselves the pleasure of it" (17). Further, as Susie Orbach stated, "women have occupied this dual role of feeding others while needing to deny themselves" and "women must hold back their desires for the cakes they bake for others and satisfy themselves with a brine canned tuna salad with dietetic trimmings" (18).

As one woman said:

> "I'm supposed to cook for everyone else, watch everyone else tuck in but stay thin. It's not fair!"

Food therefore offers a conflict, particularly for women, between eating and denial.

Guilt versus pleasure

Many foods such as chocolate, chips, sweets, and cakes are not only seen as a pleasure but can also generate feelings of guilt. In fact, advertising plays upon this with slogans such as "forbidden fruit" and "naughty but nice," and the concept of "sins of the flesh" indicates that both eating and sex are at once pleasurable and guilt-ridden activities. In her autobiography Kim Chernin clearly described her own struggles with food and the conflict between the need for food and the subsequent self-loathing. She wrote that she could not "make it as far as lunch without eating a pound of candy" and that "I ran from bakery to bakery, from street stall to street stall . . . I bought a pound of chocolate and ate it as I ran," and unable to wait her turn any longer in a queue for a hot dog behind a man who had just ordered his, "I suddenly dart forward, grab the plate and begin to run . . . I run with a sudden sense of release" (19). Similarly, Levine described in her book *I Wish I Were Thin, I Wish I Were Fat* how "I still feel as if I am sneaking food when I eat something I love. And I still feel guilty when I let it get the better of me" (20). These foods represent pleasure and fulfill a need. Their consumption is then followed by guilt and feelings of "shame," feeling "self-conscious," "frantic," and "perverse."

As one woman we interviewed said:

> "I constantly feel guilty when I'm eating something. Like I'll eat a big bar of chocolate and then I'll feel guilty. I'll eat a packet of crisps and wish I hadn't."

Similarly:

> "I had that circle of bad eating then feeling guilty about the fact that I'd eaten so much."

And another said:

> "You feel depressed you haven't got much time for yourself, so you eat a bar of chocolate, which does actually, doesn't help. But you know at that time it does. When you are actually eating it . . . it feels good. It's afterwards . . . you think, stupid woman, why did you do that?"

Food is therefore loaded with a conflict between guilt and pleasure.

Health versus pleasure

At times food can also generate a conflict between health and pleasure. Parents may well be motivated to give their children a healthy diet, and the pleasure you get when they like your home-cooked healthy meal is great. *But* it is amazing how much more pleasure they sometimes seem to get from chicken kiev and chips or a trip to the fish and chip shop, and it's hard not to occasionally give in to this just to get the pleasure of seeing them happy. As Marilyn Lawrence argued, "good nourishing food is what every mother knows her children need. She also knows that it is usually the last thing they want. Give them junk food and they will love you. But you will also have to live with the guilt about their teeth, their weight, their vitamins."

As one mother I interviewed said:

> "I'd spent 45 minutes cooking up a meal and they looked at me saying 'er what's that? That looks horrible.' But when I take them for a burger and chips they give me a hug as if I'm the best mum in the world."

Food therefore creates a conflict between health and pleasure.

Food is embedded with meanings which are often linked to our emotions and the ways in which we manage how we feel. Eating is therefore rarely driven by hunger alone and often illustrates how we have learned to use food to manage how we feel. For many, however, this can generate conflicts as the meanings are sometimes in opposition to each other.

Food and Self-Control

Food also represents self-control and thin women and men are frequently used by the media to illustrate will-power and an ability to control the desire to eat. Similarly, fasting, food refusal, and the hunger artists of the nineteenth century were and are received with a sense of wonder that people can deny themselves food. As Gordon argued, "hunger artists had no moral or religious agenda . . . their food refusal was a sheer act of will and self-control for its own sake" (21). Further, Arthur Crisp, a psychiatrist, compared the anorexic to the ascetic in terms of her "discipline, frugality, abstinence and stifling of the passions" (22), and Hilda Bruch, a psychotherapist, described the anorexic as having an "aura of special power and super human discipline" (16).

Not eating food therefore means will-power and self-control. In contrast, however, many people also show episodes of lack of control and overeating, and the overweight and obese are often used by the media to represent a lack of will-power and an inability to stand up to the powerful drive to indulge. In particular, research has identified how although dieters intend to eat less as a means to lose weight, they often show overeating in response to a range of factors, including anxiety, alcohol, and eating something they feel they should not have. This suggests that attempting not to eat paradoxically increases the probability of overeating – the specific behavior dieters are attempting to avoid. Furthermore, although those with anorexia manage to control their eating much of the time, many are prone to episodes of bingeing and overeating, and those with bulimia often switch between episodes of restriction and then periods of loss of control over their food intake. Food is therefore related to issues of control, with some showing strict control but the majority showing both control and episodes when this control is lost.

As one of our interviewees said:

> "I've got a lot of control in my life so you'd think I'd be able to control my eating but I can't, maybe it's because I'm so controlled everywhere else that I'm not controlling my eating."

Similarly another described how trying to control her diet made her eating worse:

> "It's like being a kid and being told that you can't eat that. When you've got to be an adult you can do exactly what you want . . . I mean if they told you to eat it you wouldn't."

Many people often also think of their eating behavior as an addiction like smoking or drug taking, as they want to eat, try not to eat, then become obsessed with food:

> "I think about it all the time and it becomes an obsession and I've started waking up in the night to eat . . . and the obsession is that I know that I shouldn't be thinking it . . ."

And:

". . . I think it's like being an alcoholic and I think that's how it will have to be for me . . . so it's the price I've had to pay to lose the weight is to lose the interest in food."

Food is therefore embedded with meanings related to both emotional regulation and conflict. It also signifies control and at times the loss of this control. Therefore at times when we feel out of control of our lives, whether it is in terms of relationships, our work, or just our lives in general, many of us turn to food as a way to feel more in control. These meanings are often generated as we interact with our social worlds.

Food and Social Interaction

Food is central to the ways in which we interact with one other. We have special meals for "the birthday party" and "Sunday lunch." And festivals such as Christmas, Thanksgiving, Easter, Passover, Hanukkah, Diwali, and Ramadan all involve food and sometimes fasting which is ended with a celebratory meal. Food is also a common tool for connecting within the family and the dinner table is often the only place where the family get together to share their experiences of the day. We also eat differently with others compared to when we are alone, and there are many implicit rules about eating in company such as eating a similar amount, at a similar speed, and the same number of courses as others around us. That's why we often ask "who's having a starter?" or "who's having a pudding?" when we eat out, as to eat alone while others watch would feel strange and uncomfortable. It's also why it sends a shudder round the table when someone says "I'm not eating, I'm on a diet" or when a family member ostentatiously leaves all the food on their plate, as they are not obeying these hidden but very strong rules.

As one of our interviewees said:

"Being Latin, we talk about food when we sit around the table, the whole family . . . It's also the way I was programmed from when I was a kid. You have to finish everything on your plate so I would overcook, I would put everything on the plate and I would eat it."

In particular, food can be a symbol of family love, of power within families or society, of sexual attraction, and of religious identity.

Food means family

Food as love

Providing a meal for the family is one of the most basic ways to express love and caring, and putting time and effort into food preparation makes this love and caring seem all the more apparent. Similarly, eating food that has been carefully prepared by others is also the most basic way to accept this love and show yours in return. Therefore the simple daily exchange "dinner's on the table!" followed by "thanks mum that looks lovely!" is a central part of how families show their love for each other. As Marilyn Lawrence argued, "Food is the medium through which women demonstrate our love and concern for our children, lovers, husbands and friends" and "taking care over the preparation of food is an act of love." And that is why when children say "Err! What's that? I don't like potatoes," deep down they know that it is going to have a strong effect. Food signifies love and disrupting this is guaranteed to make an impact.

As one woman said:

> "When I first had children I was amazed at how much pleasure I got when I had cooked and my children wolfed down their food. I felt like I was such a good mother. The family felt like it was really working at last!"

Power dynamics in the family

For many centuries men have been given larger amounts of food than women, children, or the elderly, and if meat is scarce men will often be given it over the other family members. In some cases men are also served first and when food is running low the woman may well give herself the scraps so that the others can remain well nourished. Food can also therefore reflect power dynamics within a family. Even in the modern family where equality is assumed, watch who gets the "best bits" of meat or the crunchiest roast potatoes. Quite often this indicates where the power balance lies and who "wears the trousers." In my own family, my gran would give my dad the best bits of meat and the crunchiest potatoes and send him next door with a tray to have his tea in front of the TV. My sister and I were always outraged and felt this was unfair as we had to stay in the kitchen and eat at the table. Looking back, however, I suspect she just wanted to get rid of the men so that the women could get down to the real business of chatting without them!

Food as social power

Food is also a symbol of social power and social status. Up until about the 1920s all powerful men were portrayed as portly and even obese by today's standards, to signify that they had enough to eat and they were in a powerful position in society. In contrast, the poor were thin, with the look of the "consumptive," as they had less money and therefore less power. Nowadays, however, in the Western world those in powerful positions are often thin and are portrayed like this by the media. This is not to suggest that they don't have access to food *but* that they do have access but have chosen not to eat much of it. Denial and food avoidance have therefore come to symbolize having power over the social world.

For example, when political prisoners need to make a social statement they refuse to eat and start a hunger strike. Bobby Sands was a political prisoner in Northern Ireland in the 1980s and refused food as a political protest. He was voted a member of parliament by his local constituency just before he died. Similarly, the suffragettes in the early twentieth century also turned to hunger strikes as a political protest over gender inequalities. For example, Lady Constance Lytton (1869–1923) was imprisoned in Liverpool for 14 days following a suffragette demonstration. In protest, she started to scratch the words "votes for women" on her body, went on a hunger strike, and was promptly force-fed on eight occasions. She told the wardress "We are sorry if it will give you trouble: we shall give as little as possible: but our fast is against the government and we shall fight them with our lives not hurting anyone else."

In a similar way, Susie Orbach regarded eating disorders as a form of "hunger strike" as women refuse to eat as a means to claim back some power in their worlds. The presence of food therefore represents social power and the denial of food is a powerful tool for regaining control over the world.

Food and sexuality

Some foods are also linked with sex and sexuality. Advertisements for ice cream offer their product as the path to sexual fulfillment; chocolate is often consumed in an erotic fashion; and the best-selling book *The Joy of Sex* by Alex Comfort was named after the *Joy of Cooking* and was subtitled "A gourmet guide to love making." This relationship between food and sex is central to many cultures and has been throughout history. Rite of passage ceremonies marking the onset of sexuality involve practices such as washing with the blood of a goat and killing the first animal, and eating red meat is often considered to arouse sexual desire. For example, history tells us that a captain of a slave ship stopped eating meat to prevent him from lusting after female slaves. Similarly, low meat diets were recommended in the nineteenth and twentieth centuries to discourage masturbation in young males.

Further, sexual language describing women or sex is often derived from animals or foods, such as "beaver," "bird," "bitch," "chick," "lamb," "meat market," "beef," and "beefy" (23). At a more prosaic level, "going out for dinner," "a dinner for two," and "a candlelit dinner" are frequent precursors to sex. Imagine what you would cook for someone you fancied who was coming round for dinner for the first time – it is more difficult than it seems. A roast dinner could seem too "motherly," oysters would be too desperate, and beans on toast would look like you couldn't be bothered!

Food can therefore reflect sexuality and symbolizes the individual as a sexual being.

Food and religious identity

Food is also embedded with meanings associated with religion and religious identity. Many religions such as Islam, Judaism, and Hinduism involve rules as to which foods can and cannot be eaten and the ways in which foods can be combined. In addition, religious ceremonies and festivals are recognized through food preparation and food sharing, whether it is the turkey at Christmas or chocolate eggs at Easter for Christians, or feasts on holy days such as Eid at the end of Ramadan for Muslims. Therefore, eating food, preparing food, and providing food for others becomes a medium through which holiness can be communicated within the family, and a sign of religious identity and religiosity.

Food is therefore central to many forms of social interaction and there are many implicit rules about how we should eat in company compared to on our own. Food also reflects family love, power dynamics within the family, and power within the broader social context, and is central to our notions of sexuality and religious identity. Therefore, when these rules are broken through overeating or undereating in public, a sudden shock wave can be felt as we quickly recognize that something is wrong. And even if we see someone who is overweight or underweight, these shock waves are still felt as we can tell they have violated these rules even if we haven't seen them doing it.

Food as Self-Identity and Communication

Food has many meanings in terms of emotional regulation, conflict, control, and social interaction. Central to all these meanings is food as a vehicle for communication. Food can be used to make statements about "Who am I?" "How am I feeling?" "What do I feel about you?" and "How do you make me feel?" People can use food to make statements about their emotions ("I am fed up," "I am bored"), about how they feel about other people ("I love you," "I appreciate you"), and about how others make them feel ("You make me feel sexy," "You make me feel loved"). They can also use food to communicate that things are going wrong ("I am unhappy," "I feel unloved," "I need to be looked after"). And because food is used in this way we quickly learn to "read" what someone is saying through the way they eat. So when we see someone refusing to eat we know they are saying "I am unhappy"; when they cook us a lovely meal we know they mean "I care about you"; and when they buy us a box of chocolates we read this as "you are special."

Food plays many roles in our lives (© Adam Merrin)

So when we are feeding our children as they grow up, we are teaching them the meaning of food and they are learning to read what food means and what we mean when we give them the food we give them. Then when they grow up and want to make a statement about who they are or how they are feeling, the chances are that food will make up part of this statement.

Imagine the following scenario between a mum and a daughter:

DAUGHTER: Mummy I had a horrible day today. Amy wouldn't play with me.
MUM: Let's have some cake to cheer us up!
DAUGHTER AND MUM: Oo this cake is lovely.

The daughter is learning that cake is a great way to manage her emotions. She is also learning that eating cake makes her and her mum feel close. And she is learning that her mum believes eating cake to manage your emotions is a good thing. Then as she grows up she may well use food to manage her emotions more and more. This can lead to feelings of conflict as she could become overweight, then feel guilty for eating too much. *But* if she tries to eat less she may well become unhappy as she hasn't learned

> ### Take home points
>
> - Food is not just about hunger but about a wide range of meanings.
> - We use food to manage our emotions and eat when we are bored, fed up, want to celebrate, or as a treat.
> - Food can create conflicts between guilt and pleasure, the desire to eat and the desire to stay thin, the desire to be healthy and the need for pleasure.
> - Overeating is seen as a sign of lack of control, whereas not eating can symbolize will-power.
> - Food is central to how we interact with others and is used to show love, to celebrate family life, culture, and religion.
> - We use food to make statements about who we are and to communicate how we would like to be seen by others.

other ways to manage her feelings. *And* she might feel distanced from her mum if they can no longer connect over food. *And* if she doesn't eat cake with her mum, her mum may well read this as rejection. *And* she knows that if she eats less and less her mum will read this as indicating that something is very wrong and that she is upset. So food becomes a very powerful way of managing and communicating emotions rather than using words.

All over a piece of cake!

So it is fine to do this once in a while. But it is also good to encourage children to find other ways to manage their emotions, particularly by talking about their feelings. Then in the future when they are upset, food won't be their main source of support. *Then* they won't overeat as a means to make themselves feel better *or* undereat in order to show the world that they are having problems.

In Summary

In times of hardship and famine, food means health and staying alive. But for those where food is freely available the meanings of food have become wide-ranging as food takes on an increasingly complex role in our lives.

For example, food is linked with emotional regulation as people eat to manage stress or when they are bored or fed up. It also generates conflicts between eating, denial, guilt, and pleasure. Furthermore, food is embedded with issues of control, reflected in times of over- and undereating, and it is central to the ways in which we interact with others. It can be used to show love and affection within relationships, as a sign of power, or as a symbol of sexuality or religious identity. Finally, food is often a way to make statements about who we are, how we feel about others, and how they make us feel. For the majority, all these meanings are part and parcel of the day-to-day process of choosing which foods we like, which ones we are going to eat, and how we are going to feed others. For the minority, however, these complex meanings of food can result in eating becoming a destructive and damaging form of behavior, resulting in either obesity or eating disorders. These are described in Chapters 5–8.

4

Why are eating habits so hard to change?

Have you ever tried to give up smoking, exercise more, drink less, stop saying peculiar little phrases that slip out without thinking, or change your hairstyle or the kinds of clothes you wear? We are creatures of habit who generally like our routines and rituals and feel safest in our comfort zones. Eating behavior is no different and most of the ways we eat and the foods we like have been learned from an early age and involve the minimal amount of thought and effort. They feel almost instinctual. And that's how habits feel – almost instinctual. So we clean our teeth every morning without planning to and because if we didn't it would feel wrong. We put our deodorant on often without even knowing we have done so and we choose our breakfast without any hesitation.

This chapter will discuss the following:

- How do habits develop?
- Why are habits difficult to change?
- How do some people change their behavior?
- How can habits be broken?

How Do Habits Develop?

It's Monday morning. The alarm clock goes and you drag yourself out of bed. You make your way downstairs and through half-closed eyes flick the kettle on, put the tea bag in your favorite mug, put two pieces of bread in

The Good Parenting Food Guide: Managing What Children Eat without Making Food a Problem, First Edition. Jane Ogden.
© 2014 John Wiley & Sons, Ltd. Published 2014 by John Wiley & Sons, Ltd.

Good parenting . . .

Habits are formed through repetition, reinforcement, and association and can be very hard to change. Parenting is about creating good habits in our children. Parenting around food helps to create healthy eating habits that will carry on throughout our children's lives. And much of parenting is also about being a good role model, which sometimes means changing our own habits into ones which we would like our children to copy.

the toaster, and get the Marmite out. Well that's what I do and have been doing since I was about 14. You might have a shower first, you might have cereal, or porridge, or muesli, or a boiled egg. And if you are Japanese you might have rice, or a strong espresso and a pastry if you are Italian. But most of us will do this with very little thought or conscious decision making. On a Saturday morning we might think "what shall I have today?" but on a Monday we use the smallest amount of thought and processing capacity possible. And then we find that we are dressed, have cleaned our teeth, and are nagging the children to speed up without quite knowing where the morning has gone or how this has all happened. These are habits and they require very little thinking having been bedded down over many years of doing exactly the same thing over and over again. And most of what we eat, how we eat, and how much we eat is also a habit and has become entrenched from a very early age.

Habits are formed through three very simple processes: repetition, reinforcement, and association. When we repeat a behavior several times it quickly becomes a pattern. It then becomes a habit if it is reinforced by something positive such as we like doing it, someone else likes us doing it, or it makes us feel good. This is even true for "bad habits" as these also make us feel good at some level or another. Then the behavior becomes a strong habit if it becomes associated with something in our environment or our inner mood. So take teeth cleaning. We clean our teeth every morning because as children our mum nagged us to do it. After a while this repetitive behavior became a pattern. Then it became a habit because we like it, it makes our breath feel fresher, forgetting to do it makes us uncomfortable and sometimes people tell us "your breath smells." Finally, we then learned to associate cleaning our teeth with walking past the bathroom, the sound of someone else cleaning theirs, the smell of tooth-paste, or the last task to do before coming back downstairs in the morning. We have a habit and not doing it leaves us with a sense that something is not quite right. And this feeling that something isn't right is just uncomfort-able enough for us to want to keep carrying on with our habit.

For breakfast it's the same pattern. Lots of people don't like breakfast as they are "too tired," "it makes me feel sick," or "I just can't eat in the morning." This is because their normal behavior is not to eat and eating feels strange. But then get them to eat breakfast every morning for a couple of weeks and soon a new pattern will be set (repetition). They will start to like the feeling of being more alert and spending a few minutes each morning sitting quietly eating (reinforcement), and this new behavior will be triggered by seeing the fridge, smelling someone else's toast, or simply getting out of bed (association). Then, not eating breakfast will start to feel strange as their new normal behavior has been established.

These habits, whether they be teeth cleaning or eating, are all established from a very early age and become so entrenched in our daily lives and the things we say about ourselves that they require very little thought or effort to do but a lot of effort to change.

Why Are Habits Difficult to Change?

Habits are difficult to change because ultimately at the moment of carrying out any behavior its benefits outweigh the costs. So although smoking might cause lung cancer, at the moment of having a cigarette the immediate feeling of stress leaving your body far outweighs the risk of dying in 20 years' time. Similarly, eating cake may add to your weight problem, but at the time of eating the cake the pleasure of its taste and texture cancels out the fear of having a heart attack when you are 60. Habits are therefore the result of a simple cost/benefit analysis, and mostly we are hopeless at think-ing about the future, so that the immediate benefits pretty much always outweigh the future costs. This process is facilitated by a number of differ-ent factors as follows.

Triggers

Because habits have been created by associating the behavior with a number of triggers either in the environment (the fridge) or our mood (feeling fed up) they are difficult to break, as every time we come across this trigger we are prompted to behave in a particular way. And because habits require so little thought, much of the time we aren't even aware of what we are doing. So smokers get off the train and light up, if leaving the train is their trigger, and those who overeat eat biscuits with their afternoon cup of tea, as this feels normal and not doing so doesn't feel quite right. Such environmental triggers, however, can be avoided if we make small changes to our daily routines or change our environment. But it is the internal mood triggers which are more difficult to manage as they follow us everywhere and are hard to ignore.

Habits are triggered by things around us (© Adam Merrin)

Worry and stress

Habits are part and parcel of our everyday normal lives and therefore when we don't clean our teeth, eat breakfast, have our morning coffee, or have biscuits in the afternoon we feel unsettled and slightly stressed. This feeling is unpleasant and we quickly learn that it can be avoided by carrying on with our habit. Therefore stopping smoking makes people feel stressed. This stress goes away once they have a cigarette. Similarly, not eating biscuits feels unusual, but this can all be made OK with a few biscuits. And the habit carries on as it becomes the solution to the problem created when trying to change it. It's a vicious circle. But children don't smoke, and don't find this difficult, and they feel fine when they don't clean their teeth or eat breakfast. So it's the change in the habit which makes us feel stressed *not* the absence of the actual behavior. And if we start to realize that the feeling of stress or worry is just "withdrawal" and will only be made worse in the longer term if we give in and use the habit to get rid of it, then we can start to break the habit itself.

Scripts in our heads

From an early age we develop scripts in our heads of what we like and don't like, who we are, and what we do. These scripts come from the people around us, particularly our parents, and tell us whether we are a good or a bad person. For example, some people have negative scripts in their heads which say "I am always late," "I'm a problem," "I'm selfish," "I never try my best," or "I'm stupid." Other people may have more positive scripts which tell them "I am kind," "I am thoughtful," "I work hard," "I always stick at things," or "I'm clever." These scripts can make it very difficult for us to change our habits, if we tell ourselves "I am addicted to smoking," "I have a problem with food," "cigarettes are the only way I can relax," "eating is my only crutch in life," or "I have an addictive personality." Although some of these scripts may feel "true" and reflect how people actually behave, they make it more difficult to change as breaking a longstanding habit not only means changing the behavior but also changing the very way in which a person sees themselves. And this is hard.

Social pressure

We live in a social world and spend much of our time with other people. Our behaviors are therefore intricately linked with other people and are often central to the ways in which we build up our relationships. So we may have a friend at work who we go outside and smoke with, a colleague who we have cake with in the afternoon, a husband who likes to buy us chocolates as a treat, or children who we enjoy taking out for ice cream. If we then try to change our behavior, these other people in our lives may well object and the pressure will be on to behave the way we always have done. Husbands will feel rejected if we don't eat the chocolates, our friend will feel lonely smoking on her own and we will miss out on the gossip, and ice cream will seem less of a treat. People like us to carry on the way we always have done as it makes them feel safe. If we change, then they feel that they have to change too and that is unsettling. So the social pressure always increases to maintain the status quo whenever anyone tries to break a habit. I remember a woman once who was part of my research and trying to lose weight. Her rather unpleasant husband wanted her to lose weight and used to say "here comes the elephant" when she got ready for bed. She went on a diet and was doing really well. Then suddenly he started to buy her chocolates! I think she left him!

Denial

When people try to change their habits they are mostly attempting to stop doing something they still want to do. So those stopping smoking still like smoking but know they shouldn't smoke, people on a diet like chips but try not to eat them, and those trying to be active would rather be on the sofa but try to drag themselves off to an aerobics class. This makes changing behavior difficult because it always introduces an element of denial and human beings are hopeless at denying themselves something if they want it and it is available. Furthermore, the process of denial makes the behavior we are trying to deny ourselves even more attractive and desirable than it was before. So if we say to ourselves "today I will not eat cake," automatically we think about cake more, not less. Then, because we are thinking about cake more, but can't have it, we want it more as the day progresses. Eventually when we give in and have cake, not only do we now want it more than we did in the morning, we end up eating more cake because we have been denying ourselves all day. This is a very powerful effect which means that by making food forbidden and putting ourselves into denial we paradoxically become more preoccupied, and when we do give in (which most people do) we paradoxically eat more than if we hadn't denied ourselves in the first place.

In summary, habits are difficult to change because they have often been entrenched for a very long time. They demonstrate a simple cost/benefit analysis and at the time of carrying out the behavior the immediate benefits will always outweigh the longer-term costs. In addition, changing habits is made even more difficult due to environmental triggers, the stress and worry generated when we try to change, social pressure from others who want us to carry on as usual, and the problem of denial.

Success Stories

Some people do, however, manage to change their behavior. This section will tell the stories of people who have changed their diet in order to highlight some of the ways in which success can be achieved.

Persistence

The mantra "try, try, try again" seems to be true and evidence shows that those who eventually break a habit, and change their behavior, have tried many times in the past. In my studies of success stories, people who have lost weight and kept it off have simply been more persistent than those who have regained their lost weight or not lost weight in the first place.

Life events

Changing behavior often seems to happen after people have experienced a life event of some sort. This may be a relationship breakdown, a change of job, moving house, having a health problem, or simply going on holiday. Then, as a result, the normal pattern of life is shaken up and habits can be broken more easily. For example, one man who had lost about 10 stone in weight described how this had happened after he had split up with his "monster of a girlfriend":

> "Before we split up, I would be happy, then we would have a row or something and I would think, oh I can't be bothered, I will go out and eat McDonald's."

But then after they split up, he said:

> "I was back home with my family, I was seeing my friends a lot more . . . I wanted to look good. I wanted to look good naked, that's what I used to say to myself."

The life event had taken away his need to overeat (as he was no longer rowing with his girlfriend) and it had changed where he lived and who he was living with.

Specific events therefore seem to make it easier to break a habit. In part this is because they can shake up the pattern of our lives. It is also, however, because they offer up an opportunity to reinvent who we are and redefine ourselves in better and healthier ways.

Changing the environment

Life events may help behavior change through changing our environment. But we don't always need a life event to make this happen and changes in behavior often occur as a result of simple changes to the world around us. I eat Marmite with my toast every morning without thinking. When we have run out, I have honey. If we never bought Marmite again then honey would become my new habit. You could have a white baguette every lunchtime, but if they suddenly offered only brown baguettes, you might complain at first, but soon this would become your new way of eating. Similarly, commuters might grab a coffee on the platform each morning, but if they started to sell only tea or hot chocolate this could quickly become the new norm. Simple changes in the environment can be an easy way to break a habit and change behavior.

Symptoms

Mostly, people do not think about their health until they are ill. So cigarette packets which say "smoking kills" can be ignored by the 16-year-old who feels fine, and threats of a heart attack mean nothing to the overweight 40-year-old who can still carry out their day-to-day life. But symptoms such as breathlessness, getting a headache, not being able to run for a bus, not fitting into jeans, or stomach pains can make health more of an issue and it is at these times that people are more likely to change their behavior. So smokers mostly think of giving up when the doctor listens to their chest and says "I can hear you are a smoker. Your lungs are starting to crackle," or when the lift is broken and they find the stairs difficult. And overweight people are more successful at changing their diet after struggling to do up their shoelaces or to get out of the bath. It is as if we walk around with our fingers in our ears for most of our lives not listening to any health messages coming our way. But a real live symptom that we feel in the here and now can bring us up short and be the trigger we need to change the way we behave.

Seeing behavior as the problem

Many people who are overweight believe in a biological cause to their weight problem, saying "it runs in my family," "I have a slow metabolism,"

"I was born like this," "it's my hormones," or "my diabetes makes me overweight." Similarly people who smoke say "I'm addicted," "I have an addictive personality," "I need it," or "I can't help it." Although there is some evidence that some behaviors are influenced by biology and forces beyond our control, this way of thinking does not help us change our behavior. We once had a patient who had had a heart attack which he believed was caused by "doing too much." He was then told that in order to prevent another heart attack he had to "do more exercise." He didn't follow this advice. That was because the solution being offered to him did not make sense given his beliefs about the cause of his problem. He believed he should "be doing less." In order for people to change their behavior they have to believe that their behavior is a problem. But if those who are overweight think their weight problem is caused by genetics, and smokers believe they smoke because they are addicted, then why should they change what they do?

Hope

The final factor that seems to relate to successful behavior change is hope. Most people carry on their day-to-day lives in a habitual and routinized way and see their future lives as being very much like the past and present. This is fine for those who are healthy and happy, and can lead to contentment and well-being. But for those who are not, it leads to getting stuck. One way out of being stuck is to find a sense of hope that there is another possible future out there which is different and better than the one that has been mapped out for years. One of our patients described to us the moment she realized there was hope that her future could be better than her past, and it involved seeing an image of her body during a bone scan for cancer:

> "My orthopedic surgeon got a bone scan 'cos of my tumor and then he's like my body there and there's me, there's all my fat and he goes to the kids 'look there's a little mummy in there trying to get out.' You know there is a little me here . . . seeing it on the bone scan yeah there's me and there's the big me . . . that's when I decided to go for it."

For this woman, the image of the "little me" version of herself gave her hope, which in turn resulted in her changing her behavior and losing weight. For some, hope can come from hearing other people's success stories, taking full credit for times in their own lives when they have changed their behavior, or monitoring behavior in order to find small signs of change which can be used as hopeful indicators that change is possible.

Breaking habits is hard, yet some people do manage to change their behavior. For many this seems to be after years of trying and can often happen after a life event which gives them a chance to reinvent themselves by shaking up the routines of their life. Behavior change also occurs after small and simple changes to the environment, having a symptom which raises the salience of health and well-being, seeing behavior as the problem, and gaining some hope that the future can be different from the past and present. These examples illustrate how breaking a habit is difficult but not impossible. They also highlight many ways in which as parents we can start to change not only our own unhealthy habits but also those of our children.

How Can Habits Be Changed?

So far this chapter has covered the following factors.

Habits are made through:
- Repetition
- Reinforcement
- Association

Habits are sustained by:
- A simple cost/benefit analysis
- Triggers
- Worry and stress
- Scripts in our head
- Social pressure
- Denial

People who change their behavior:
- Persist
- Experience life events
- Change their environment
- Experience symptoms
- See behavior as the problem
- Have hope

Many of these factors directly illustrate how habits can be broken and new healthier habits can be formed for parents and their children. Parenting is about creating good habits in our children and changing our own behavior so that we can be good role models for them. Here are some ideas for how to change your own behavior or that of your child. More tips can be found in the second section of this book, relating to healthy eating in general (Chapter 10), being more active (Chapter 11), overeating (Chapter 12), or undereating (Chapter 13).

Get into good habits early

Persist

"If at once you don't succeed, try, try, try again." Repetition is the key to setting up a habit. It is also the key to breaking a habit and starting a new one. Children will eventually eat what you eat. Even if they turn their noses up the first time you give them mushrooms in their spaghetti bolognese or brown toast for breakfast, persist and soon they will give in as these new foods will become familiar to them and new habits will be formed.

Be a good role model

Change your own diet first and eat in front of them making positive noises about how nice the food is. So if you want them to eat more vegetables, you need to eat them and comment on how nice they are. Soon they will start to copy you.

Say the right things

Reinforcement is a very powerful process so when they try new foods make a fuss and say "how grown up you are trying something new," and when they don't finish it say "that's so good that you tried it." Then when you are eating healthily speak positively about the foods you want them to eat, saying "these vegetables are really juicy" and "I'm quite hungry, I think I'll have an apple." All this praise will start to help them see that healthy eating is a good thing as it brings reward from their parents. Also make positive statements about the kind of eater your child is. So don't say "you are such a fussy eater," "you eat huge amounts," or "you don't seem to like your food." But find the right time to say positive things about your child. That way these positive phrases will start to become the scripts inside their head which will set them up for life, and although they won't ever quite know why, they will know that they are the kind of person who "tries everything," "knows when they are hungry," "is healthy," and "isn't fussy."

Make small changes

The easiest way to change a habit is to do it through substitution and changes so small that you can trick your mind or the minds of others into thinking that everything is the same as it always has been. Large changes involving herbal concoctions, artichokes, fennel, lentils, seeds, and nuts won't last more than a few days if at all. But small changes are much more likely to be sustained in the longer term. So drink skimmed milk rather than whole milk, squash rather than fizzy drinks, eat brown pasta, bread, and rice rather than white, and add hidden vegetables into familiar food rather than confronting your children with new vegetables all in one go. Then cook them their familiar pasta dish, with brown pasta rather than white, and add a new vegetable on the side and see what happens.

Change the environment

You are in charge of the car and the money and do the shopping and the cooking. Therefore manage their environment in ways that make it easier for them to develop healthy habits. So if they have got into the habit of drinking gallons of fizzy drink when they get in from playing football, stop buying fizzy drinks and get some squash or juice instead. They may complain at first but soon they will be swigging this back and the old habit will have been forgotten. Similarly, don't have a cupboard full of crisps or sweets for them to graze on while waiting for their tea, but make sure you always have a fruit bowl on display with bananas, apples, and grapes for them to grab as they walk past. And as they grow up you may have less and less control over what they eat outside the house, but you still have control over what they eat in it.

Use social pressure

Children want to be like their parents and will eventually eat what you eat. But even more powerful is the desire to be like their friends. So have children back for tea and use this as a chance to introduce new foods to your child. Similarly when they go to a friend's house and the friend's mum asks "what do they eat?" say "give them whatever you are having" as the chances are they will eat it at someone else's house even if they won't eat it at home. Use social pressure to your advantage, and rather than playing safe with familiar foods cooked in familiar ways when the pattern of your meal is changed by having someone new there, change the pattern of what you eat and get your child to try and eat foods just because their friends are doing the same.

Use life events

Many people change their behavior after a life event which disrupts their routines. If you are thinking about changing a habit, then a good time to try is when the daily routine has already been changed by something that has happened in your life. This could be a more serious event such as a family illness, change of school, or house move. But it could also be simple things such as having family to stay for the weekend, going away on holiday, coming back from holiday, changing the school routine, or even trying out the new supermarket or buying a new kitchen table. Anything different challenges our day-to-day habits without us realizing it and this is a good time to introduce new ways of eating into the household.

Make plans

When we behave spontaneously we think less and act out of habit. Therefore we buy the same foods from the supermarket and cook the same foods for tea as this is the easiest path to take. But to change a habit requires effort

Take home points

- Most of us are creatures of habit and eating is one of these habits.
- Habits are made through repetition, reinforcement, and association.
- They are difficult to change and are sustained by a number of factors.
- Triggers in the environment, feeling worried when we change a behavior, scripts in our heads, pressure from others, and denial all help to keep a bad habit going.
- Habits can be changed with effort.
- You need to persist, make small changes, use social pressure, take advantage of times when things have changed, use social pressure, and make plans.
- Also be a good role model, say the right things, and change the environment.

and this involves planning. Therefore, if you decide that the family needs to eat more healthily, write down seven menus for the next week, turn this into a shopping list, and shop armed with a set of plans for the week ahead. Then stick the menus on the fridge and use them. Once plans are made they are easy to stick to, particularly if they are clear and detailed. And they are even easier to stick to if you tell others about them and get the family involved. Some menu suggestions can be found in Chapter 9.

In Summary

Much of what we do is a matter of habit, which can be very difficult to change. Habits are formed by repetition, reinforcement, and association and involve very little effort and thought, and are great when time is short and we have lots of other things on our minds. They are sustained by many factors such as the scripts in our heads, the feelings of worry or stress when something is different, and the paradoxical effect of denial which can make us preoccupied with the very thing we are trying not to do. But essentially a habit is maintained because at the time of doing anything, whether it be eating cake, smoking a cigarette, or cleaning our teeth, the benefits of doing it outweigh the costs. Changing habits and forming new ones can therefore be quite difficult, but this chapter has outlined some simple ways forward, such as making small subtle changes rather than large obvious ones, using social pressure to your advantage, using life events however small, being a good role model, and saying the right things. More tips for changing eating behavior are given in the second half of this book.

5

Overweight and obesity
Prevalence, consequences, and causes

There are many different problems relating to eating behavior but the most common relate to overeating and subsequent weight gain. This chapter will cover being overweight and obese in terms of the following:

- What is overweight or obesity?
- How common is it?
- What are the consequences of being overweight?
- What are the causes of being overweight or obese?

Magazines, newspapers, and TV programs are full of articles and items about weight gain in children and adults, and there is no denying that obesity is more common than it used to be. So how are overweight and obesity defined? How common are they and why has there been this increase?

What Is Obesity?

Although we frequently use the terms "being overweight" and "obesity," defining these terms is not as straightforward as you would expect, as any measure needs to take into account the ratio between height and weight (i.e. taller people are simply heavier), age (the ratio is different for children and adults), and health (muscle weighs more than fat but is not bad for you). The simplest way of assessing whether or not a person is

The Good Parenting Food Guide: Managing What Children Eat without Making Food a Problem, First Edition. Jane Ogden.
© 2014 John Wiley & Sons, Ltd. Published 2014 by John Wiley & Sons, Ltd.

Good parenting . . .

Obesity is on the increase in a world which can make gaining weight easy and staying thin a struggle. Good parenting is about giving our children healthy eating habits from an early age so that they eat a healthy diet without over- or undereating. It is also about encouraging them to have an easy approach to food where it is a pleasure without being an obsession. A lifetime feeling fat is miserable in a world that values thinness, and a lifetime being fat can result in a non-stop battle with weight and a history of failed dieting.

overweight or obese is through using Body Mass Index (BMI), which is a ratio between height and weight. The equation is weight (kg) divided by height (m²). You can use the following link to find a simple BMI calculator: http://pediatrics.about.com/cs/usefultools/l/bl_bmi_calc.htm. Using this approach the following definitions are used for adults:

- Normal weight: BMI 18.5–24.9
- Overweight: BMI 25.0–29.9
- Obese: BMI 30+

For children it is more complicated as the ratio between weight and height changes as they grow. To find out if your child is overweight or obese calculate their BMI then use the BMI growth chart (see Figure 5.1 or Figure 5.2). This will enable you to see where your child fits into the population. Track across and find your child's percentile and then see which category they fit into.

BMI categories for children:

- Underweight: BMI less than the 5th percentile
- Healthy weight: BMI 5th percentile up to the 85th percentile
- Overweight: BMI 85th percentile up to less than the 95th percentile
- Obese: BMI greater than or equal to the 95th percentile

This is the best way that we have at the moment of assessing whether or not your child is a healthy weight. As you can see, there is a very wide range

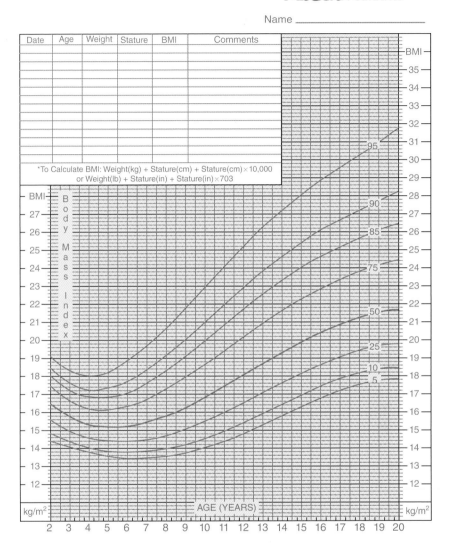

About. Pediatrics

Name _____

Date	Age	Weight	Stature	BMI	Comments

*To Calculate BMI: Weight(kg) ÷ Stature(cm) ÷ Stature(cm) × 10,000
or Weight(lb) ÷ Stature(in) ÷ Stature(in) × 703

Figure 5.1 Body mass index-for-age percentiles, 2 to 20 years: girls
Source: Child growth charts (girls). National Center for Health Statistics in collaboration with the National Center for Chronic Disease Prevention and Health Promotion (2000). http://www.cdc.gov/growthcharts, p. 53.

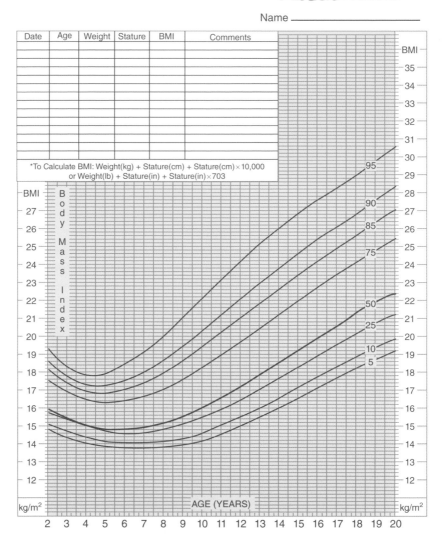

Figure 5.2   Body mass index-for-age percentiles, 2 to 20 years: boys
Source: Child growth charts (boys). National Center for Health Statistics in
collaboration with the National Center for Chronic Disease Prevention and
Health Promotion (2000). http://www.cdc.gov/growthcharts, p. 52.

for "healthy weight" which covers 80 centiles. This is to account for differences in fat and muscle composition, bone density, and ethnic differences. Therefore if your child does fall into the underweight, overweight, or obese categories it does really mean that they have a problem with their weight.

How Common Is Obesity?

Since about 1970 adults and children have generally become heavier in most countries of the world.

Adults

The rates of adult obesity in the UK increased dramatically from 1993 to about 2007 but have been relatively stable for the past five or six years. If obesity is defined as a BMI greater than 30, reports show that in the UK in 1980, 6 percent of men and 8 percent of women were obese, and that this had increased to 13 percent and 16 percent respectively in 1994 and to 22 percent and 24 percent in 2009. In 2009 the average BMI was 27 for both men and women.

Estimates for the USA suggest that roughly half of American adults are overweight, that a third are obese, and that women have grown particularly heavier in recent years. Across the world, the World Health Organization estimates that 1.5 billion adults worldwide are overweight and 400 million are obese. The highest rates of obesity are found in Tunisia, the USA, Saudi Arabia, and Canada, and the lowest are found in China, Mali, Japan, Sweden, and Brazil; the UK, Australia, and New Zealand are all placed in the middle of the range. Across Europe, people in Northern and Western Europe are thinner than in Eastern and Southern Europe and women are more likely to be obese than men.

Children

In England, in 1994 data showed that 9 percent of boys and 13.5 percent of girls were overweight and 1.7 percent of boys and 2.6 percent of girls were obese. These figures were more than 50 percent higher than 10 years earlier, and by 2010 the numbers had risen to 25 percent of boys and 33 percent of girls who were overweight or obese. The prevalence of overweight children worldwide has doubled or tripled in the past 20 years in the following countries: Australia, Brazil, Canada, Chile, Finland, France, Germany, Greece, Japan, the UK, and the USA. Globally, the number of overweight children under the age of 5 in 2010 was estimated to be over 42 million, with close to 35 million of these living in developing countries. For example, even though the rates are low in China and Japan, they are steadily increasing. Reports indicate that the prevalence of childhood obesity has tripled in Japan and that 1 in 10 children in China are now obese.

There is also a literature exploring whether childhood obesity tracks into adulthood. One study suggested that being an overweight child does not necessarily mean that you will be an overweight adult (24). Several studies, however, do show a strong link between weight in childhood and later life. For example, researchers explored the tracking of obesity in a London school-based sample and showed that if a child was overweight or obese by age 11 this persisted until age 16 (25). Similarly, a review of 10 studies concluded that obesity by age 2 years predicted obesity in later life. A study in 2005 also reported that obesity by age 7 years was predicted by very early life risk factors including birth weight, infant BMI, catch-up growth, as well as parental obesity, time spent watching television, and shorter sleep duration (26).

It is therefore clear that childhood obesity is increasingly common and seems to have a strong link with weight in later life.

What Are the Consequences of Being Overweight or Obese?

Obesity has several consequences and can cause both psychological and physical health problems.

Psychological problems

For children, the most immediate consequences of being overweight or obese are psychological as we currently live in a world where being thin is valued and being overweight is stigmatized and associated with a host of negative attributes. In the late 1960s, researchers showed groups of 5- and 10-year-old children drawings of different-sized adults. The adults were thin, medium, or overweight. The children were then asked to describe what kind of person the adult would be. The children associated the medium-sized adults with all positive qualities and the thin and fat adults with all negative qualities (27). In a further experiment, the researchers presented the children with drawings of children who were disabled in different ways, such as having crutches and a leg brace, an amputated forearm, or a facial disfigurement, together with an obese child. The children were then asked to "tell me which boy (girl) you like the best." All the children rated the obese child as the one they liked least.

In general, research shows that children associate obesity with being lazy, dirty, stupid, ugly, cheats, and liars (28). In addition, obesity is often seen as the fault of the child and it is assumed that the obese have brought their size upon themselves through overeating, a lack of control, or other emotional problems. This all contributes to the negative beliefs children hold about obesity. In fact, children seem to develop negative beliefs about the obese as early as 6 years of age, and these beliefs remain relatively constant through to adulthood. As a result of all these negative stereotypes, children who are overweight or obese often show psychological problems as a response to the reactions of those around them. In particular, they may experience low self-esteem, anxiety, low mood, and a general lack of confidence. Furthermore, they are more likely to be bullied than thin children, which can lead to underachievement or missing school.

These beliefs about body size are not, however, the same across all cultures. For example, black women in Cape Town from disadvantaged communities were asked about the acceptable body size for women and children. These women placed a high value upon food as food was often scarce, and therefore regarded limiting what they ate as unacceptable. They also described increased body size as a sign of well-being and believed that larger women had happier marriages. In addition they said that overweight children were seen as a sign of health as it meant that they had access to sufficient food (29). Similarly, women from Ghana, Latin America, Puerto Rico, China, and the Philippines also believe that a higher body weight is linked with wealth and health (30).

Obesity is also associated with psychological problems in adults, and given that childhood obesity often tracks into adulthood, many of these problems probably start early on. In general, people who are obese are more likely to suffer from depression, anxiety, low self-esteem, and high levels of body dissatisfaction. In fact one study showed that obese women in the US were five times more likely to be depressed than women who were not obese (31). Another study asked people who had lost weight through surgery how they felt about their new thinner size and they reported that they would rather be deaf, dyslexic, diabetic, or have heart disease or acne than return to their former weight (32).

Physical problems

For children, the physical consequences of obesity mostly relate to being immobile and unfit and not being able to be as active as their friends and peer group. In fact, one study of children at a summer camp reported that overweight children were more likely to spend their time floating than swimming in the swimming pool compared to thinner children (33). Some health problems do start early, however, and studies show a link between being obese as a child and having childhood asthma and type 2 diabetes.

For adults, obesity is clearly associated with a wide range of physical health problems. These include cardiovascular disease, heart attacks, diabetes, joint trauma, back pain, many types of cancer, hypertension, and strokes, and the likelihood of these problems simply increases as a person's BMI gets greater than 25. The effects of obesity are also related to where the excess weight is carried, with weight stored around the middle being more harmful than weight carried on the bottom or thighs. In the UK while the prevalence of type 1 diabetes remained constant between 1996 and 2005 the prevalence of type 2 diabetes increased from 2.8 percent to 4.3 percent, which can largely be explained by the rise in obesity. Obesity is also directly linked with mortality and decreased life expectancy.

Causes of Obesity

So what causes this problem? There are three key approaches to understanding the causes of obesity, which focus on genetics, the environment, and behavior. These will now be considered.

Genetics

Size appears to run in families and the probability that a child will be overweight is related to the parents' weight. For example, having one obese parent results in a 40 percent chance of producing an obese child, and having two obese parents results in an 80 percent chance. In contrast, the probability that thin parents will produce overweight children is very small – about 7 percent. Parents and children, however, share both their environment and genetics so this similarity could be due to either factor. To address this problem, research has examined twins and adoptees. Twin studies have examined the weight of identical twins reared apart (identical genes but different environments) and the weight of non-identical twins reared together (different genes but similar environments). The results show that the identical twins reared apart are more similar in weight than the non-identical twins reared together, indicating a role for genetics. Studies also show that the weight of people who have been adopted is more similar to that of their biological parents than that of their adoptive family.

In general, researchers believe that there is a role for genetics for both weight and where body fat is stored (upper versus lower body), that a mother's weight is a better predictor of her child's weight than that of the father, and that the role of genetics becomes less important as a person's BMI gets larger.

But this cannot explain why there has been such a huge increase in the prevalence of obesity over the past 30 years, as our genes have not changed during this time. In addition, it is not clear how a genetic basis for obesity would translate into actual obesity. For example, although it is often believed that the obese have a slower metabolic rate than the non-obese, there is no evidence for this. Obesity is also often blamed on an underactive thyroid, but this, again, is not supported by the evidence. Further, it used to be believed that the obese simply were born with more fat cells to fill up, but this has not been proven.

Finally, genetics cannot explain migration data which show very clearly that as populations move from one country to another they quickly take on the body weight of their new environment. For example, for Nigerians living in Nigeria the prevalence of obesity is 5 percent, but for those Nigerians who move to the US the rate is 39 percent. Similarly, for the Japanese living in Japan the rate of obesity is 4 percent, but for Japanese living in Brazil the rate is also 39 percent. Diabetes also shows a similar pattern. For example, for South Asians living in South Asia the rate of diabetes is 13 percent, but the rate rises to 18 percent for those South Asians living in the US; and for Samoans the rate of diabetes is 4 percent in Samoa but 20 percent for those living in the US (34). In addition, even though our body weight is similar to that of our parents it is even more similar to that of our peer group, as it seems that fatness runs in peer groups more than it runs in biological families (35).

Therefore although it would seem that obesity runs in families, and that some people might have a genetic predisposition to become obese, genetics cannot be the main cause of this problem. Researchers have therefore turned to both the environment and individual behavior as more useful explanations.

The obesogenic environment

To explain the increase in obesity, researchers have turned their attention to the role of the external world which has been labeled an "obesogenic environment" (36). For example, the food industry with its food advertising, cheap ready meals, and takeaways discourages food shopping and cooking and encourages eating out and snacking. There has also been a reduction in manual labor and an increase in the use of cars, computers, and television, which makes us more sedentary both at work and at home. And even if we want to be active, lifts and escalators prevent stair use, and towns are designed to make walking difficult due to the absence of street lights and pavements and large distances between homes and places of entertainment or shops.

We live in a world where it is easy to just sit

This obesogenic environment creates a world in which it is easy to gain weight and it requires effort to remain thin. In response to this, recent government strategies have developed initiatives such as subsidies for leisure centers, local campaigns to encourage stair climbing by putting prompts near lifts and stair wells, and legislation to modify and limit food advertising. Similarly, some companies encourage their staff to be active in their lunch breaks by organizing walking groups and offering gym facilities. And school and work canteens are supported in their attempts to offer healthier meals. In the same way that many governments have now finally responded to the knowledge that smoking kills by banning it in public places, steps are being taken to intervene at an environmental and policy level to control the obesity epidemic.

We therefore live in an obesogenic environment that makes it easy to gain weight and difficult to stay thin. For many disciplines, such as sociology or public health medicine, this would be a satisfactory answer to the question "what causes obesity?" and all interventions could be targeted at the level of the population and involve changes to the environment. However, I think that this doesn't quite work as a full explanation because although we are all living in the modern world, not everyone becomes obese. This therefore points to the role of behavior.

Individual behavior

Even if we live in an obesogenic environment, in the end weight is the result of a simple equation: energy in versus energy out. Therefore, to gain weight people must consume more energy than they use up in their day-to-day lives. Research has therefore looked at the role of diet (energy in) and physical activity (energy out).

Eating behavior   The energy in versus energy out equation is a very fine balance and even just eating one extra piece of toast per day that you don't need can result in a half-stone increase in weight after a year. Imagine how quickly this could turn into becoming overweight or obese. It is clear, therefore, that people who are overweight have eaten more than they needed in the past. It is also clear that in order to maintain this level of weight they must be eating exactly what they are using up in energy, otherwise their weight would go down. As Andrew Prentice argued, "Obesity can only occur when energy intake remains higher than energy expenditure, for an extended period of time. This is an incontrovertible cornerstone on which all explanations must be based" (37). Studies have therefore asked a series of different questions to explore how much, why, and when the overweight and obese overeat.

Do the obese eat for different reasons compared to the non-obese?   When asked why they eat, most people say "I'm hungry" or "I like it" and tend to see eating behavior as a biological need driven by the need to survive. Eating behavior, however, is much more complex than this as we eat for so many reasons other than hunger: "I was bored," I was unhappy," "It was there," "I needed to clear my plate," "Sunday lunch is a big family time," "I was out with my friends." Chapter 2 described the many ways in which we learn to like different foods and Chapter 3 described the many ways in which we use food in our lives. In the context of obesity, studies suggest that becoming overweight is specifically linked with emotional eating, external eating, and mindless eating.

Emotional eating   When a child is upset, the easiest and quickest way to calm them down is to give them food. This acts as a distraction from the feelings they are having, it gives them something to do with their hands and mouth, and it shifts their attention from whatever was upsetting them. If the food chosen is also seen as a treat, such as sweets or a biscuit, then they will feel "treated" and happier. In the moment, giving food to our children to manage their feelings and behavior is therefore effective. But in the longer term it can be harmful as they are learning that food is a good way to manage their emotions. Then as they go through life, whenever they are fed up, anxious, or even just bored they will turn to food as a means to make themselves feel better. This is known as emotional eating and studies indicate that emotional eating is linked with obesity. Unfortunately, for many people this only works in the short term as although they may briefly feel better after eating, they soon feel guilt, self-hate, and low self-esteem which in turn can cause further eating.

Mindless eating   Bags of crisps used to weigh 30 g and children used to eat these and stop. Many bags are now "grab bags" and weigh 60 g. Children do not eat the original 30 g then stop and hand them back saying "mummy I've had enough." They eat the lot – twice the amount they used to eat. We now live in a world where portion sizes are bigger, cakes are offered around at work, we have snacks in our cupboards, and there are "drive-in" fast food restaurants where we can buy thousands of calories' worth of food without even having to stop driving to eat it. And we eat it not because we are hungrier than we used to be, but because it's there. And when we are eating it, we do so without realizing that we are eating, and as a result it doesn't make us full. This is known as mindless eating.

Research shows that if you ask someone what they ate yesterday they will remember the food they registered as "meals": breakfast, lunch, and dinner. They don't remember the crisps they ate in the car on the way to work, the biscuits they had with their coffee in the morning, the cake they had in the afternoon, or the burger they grabbed on the way home. And they are even less likely to remember the "drink" they had which had more calories hidden in it than the average meal.

Recently we did a study looking at how much people ate in four different situations: in the car, watching TV, chatting to someone, or on their own. We found two important results. First, people ate more while watching TV than in any of the other situations. Second, the amount they ate while driving was unrelated to changes in their hunger. This indicates that we eat more when we are distracted, particularly when watching TV. It also indicates that if we are distracted, as when we are driving, we don't register the food we have eaten and it doesn't make us full (38).

Such mindless eating makes people overeat in an environment where food is easily available. This causes weight gain over time and can lead to obesity. What we know is that most people show mindless eating. But the obese probably eat mindlessly more than those of normal weight.

Eat me!: we eat because it's there (© Adam Merrin)

Do the obese eat more than the non-obese?   Research has also examined whether the obese eat more than the non-obese, focusing on the amount eaten, how they eat, and the type of food eaten.

The amount eaten: Measuring how much people eat is extremely problematic. If you ask people, they forget and only mention food that is considered "meals." If you watch them eating, they change how much they eat because they are being observed, and if you ask them to keep a food diary, they eat less, as they start to monitor their eating and realize when they are overeating. Further, given that it may only be an extra piece of bread per day that has caused their weight gain, it is unlikely that such small differences in diet would be picked up accurately. It has therefore proven very difficult to show conclusively that obese people eat more than non-obese people. However, laboratory research has shown that when the obese and non-obese are either over- or underfed in a controlled environment, these two groups gain or lose weight at the same rate, suggesting that the obese must eat more in order to maintain their higher weight (39). Further, if overeating is defined as "compared with what the body needs," the obese must overeat because they have excess body fat.

Eating differently: Some studies have also explored whether people who are obese eat differently compared to the non-obese. The results from this research show that those who are obese are more likely to skip breakfast, skip lunch, eat at night, report larger portion sizes at meal times, show a faster initial rate of eating, and take larger spoonfuls of food (40). All these behaviors may therefore help a person develop a weight problem.

Type of food: Over recent years, research has focused on the eating behavior of the obese not in terms of calories or the amount eaten, but more specifically in terms of the type of food eaten. Nowadays we eat less carbohydrate and proportionally more fat than we did 30 years ago. One theory of obesity is that it is linked to a diet relatively high in fat compared to carbohydrates. To support this theory, a study of 11,500 people in Scotland showed that those men and women who ate the lowest proportion of carbohydrate in their diets were up to four times more likely to be obese than those eating the highest proportion of carbohydrate (41). A similar study in Leeds also provided support for the fat proportion theory of obesity (42). This study reported that high-fat eaters who derived more than 45 percent of their energy from fat were 19 times more likely to be obese than those who derived less than 35 percent of their energy from fat. Such a high-fat diet has been argued to cause obesity in the following ways:

- It takes more energy to burn carbohydrates than fat and whereas carbohydrates are burned, fat is stored.
- Carbohydrates make you feel full faster.
- Fat does not switch off the desire to eat, making it easier to eat more and more fat without feeling full.

Therefore it would seem that obesity is caused by eating more than the body needs and that those who are overweight or obese are more likely to show emotional eating, mindless eating, to eat faster, to skip meals, and to eat more fat.

Physical activity

The energy-in/energy-out equation highlights a strong role for how much food is eaten. But equally there is also a key role for activity. The UK Department of Health recommendations for exercise are as follows:

- **Adults:** five or more days a week should include at least 30 minutes of at least moderate physical activity.
- **Children:** every day should involve at least 60 minutes of at least moderate physical activity with at least two sessions including activities to improve bone health, muscle strength, and flexibility.

Unfortunately the majority of both adults and children exercise far less than this. Research has therefore asked a series of questions concerning the link between activity and obesity.

Is the obesity epidemic linked to decreases in activity?   It is clear that recent increases in the rates of obesity coincide with people becoming less active due to all the factors in our obesogenic environment described above, such as cars, escalators, lifts, computers, television, and a desk-based society. For example, only 20 percent of men and 10 percent of women in the UK are employed in active occupations, and for many people leisure times are dominated by inactivity. In addition, whereas the average viewer in the 1960s watched 13 hours of television per week, in England this had doubled to 26 hours per week. Overall, data indicate that the majority of people do not meet the recommended targets for activity, that people tend to get less active as they get older, and that men are more active than women, particularly when young, but watch more TV than women as they get older. This is further exacerbated by the increased use of videos and computer games by both children and adults. In 1995, researchers presented data on changes in physical activity from 1950 to 1990 and commented: "it seems reasonable to conclude that the low levels of physical activity now prevalent in Britain must play an important, perhaps dominant role in the development of obesity by greatly reducing energy needs" (43).

Teenagers can become very sedentary

Does being sedentary predict weight gain?   To address the relationship between activity levels and weight gain a large Finnish study of 12,000 adults showed that being inactive at the start of the study was the best predictor of weight gain five years later (44). Similarly, a recent study of 146 identical twins showed that although the twins shared the same genetic makeup, the more active twin gained less weight over a 30-year period than the less active twin (45). It would therefore seem that being active protects against weight gain and that an inactive lifestyle causes overweight and obesity.

Take home points

- Obesity and being overweight are on the increase in both adults and children.
- Over a quarter of children in most Western countries are now overweight.
- Being overweight is linked to psychological problems such as teasing, anxiety, depression, low self-esteem, and poor body confidence.
- It is linked with physical illnesses in childhood such as asthma, diabetes, and feeling tired.
- Childhood obesity is linked with adult obesity which causes heart disease, cancer, back and knee pain, and shortened life expectancy.
- Obesity runs in families and has a genetic component *but* this is not the whole story.
- Obesity relates to the obesogenic environment which makes it easy to gain weight and hard to stay thin.
- Obesity is linked with overeating, often through emotional eating or mindless eating.
- It is also linked with being sedentary and a lack of exercise.

Do the obese exercise less?   Research has also examined whether the obese exercise less than the non-obese. Using time-lapse photography, an early study in the 1960s observed girls on a summer camp and reported that during swimming the obese girls spent less time swimming and more time floating, and while playing tennis the obese girls were inactive for 77 percent of the time, compared with the girls of normal weight who were inactive for only 56 percent of the time (33). Research also indicates that the obese walk less on a daily basis than the non-obese, are more sedentary during the week and weekend, and are less likely to use stairs or walk up escalators. One study explored the relationship between body weight and floor of residence in nearly 3,000 normal-weight adults across eight European cities (46). The results showed that for men, higher floor was associated with lower BMI. This association was not found for women. The authors concluded that daily stair climbing may reduce weight and therefore should be encouraged. Why the association was not there for women is unclear.

In Summary

It is clear that we are getting larger as a population and that weight problems in adults and children are far more common than they were 30 years ago. Obesity has many psychological consequences such as depression, low self-esteem, and anxiety, and for children it can be linked with friendship problems, bullying, and missing school. It is also linked with a host of physical health problems including heart disease, diabetes, cancer, and stroke, and even in childhood those who are overweight show the signs of these diseases, as well as being immobile, unfit, and unable to join in activities with friends.

In terms of the question "what causes obesity?" we know the following:

- Obesity has a strong genetic component, but this cannot explain the recent epidemic, nor can it explain migration data which show that populations quickly adopt the weight of the country they have moved to.
- We now live in an obesogenic environment which makes it easy to gain weight and hard to stay thin due to changes in town designs, occupations, increased technology, and daily habits.
- Obesity is also clearly linked to two key behaviors: eating and physical activity.
- People who are obese may show higher levels of emotional eating and mindless eating. They eat more than they need, may eat faster and skip meals, and may eat relatively more fat.
- Obesity is also linked with becoming more sedentary as a population, and those who are obese may exercise less, with low levels of activity predicting weight gain in later life.

The next chapter explores how obesity and overweight can be prevented through changes to the environment and changing the energy-in/energy-out balance by eating less and becoming more active. Tips for encouraging your child to be more active can be found in Chapter 11. Tips for encouraging healthy eating and preventing overeating can be found in Chapters 10 and 12.

6

Overweight and obesity
Prevention and treatments

The previous chapter described being overweight or obese in terms of definitions, prevalence, consequences, and causes. It described how gaining weight relates to the changing environment and two key behaviors: overeating and becoming more sedentary. In addition, it highlighted the implications of excess weight for health both in childhood and in later life.

This chapter will cover being overweight and obese in terms of:

- How can weight problems be prevented?
- How can weight problems be treated?

How Can We Prevent Obesity?

Preventing obesity involves tackling the environment and working out ways to encourage people to eat less and become more active.

Changing the environment

A public health approach to obesity involves targeting populations and trying to change the obesogenic environment. Possible public health approaches include:

- **Advertising:** Adverts for high-fat foods could contain health warnings or be restricted or banned in line with cigarette adverts.

The Good Parenting Food Guide: Managing What Children Eat without Making Food a Problem, First Edition. Jane Ogden.
© 2014 John Wiley & Sons, Ltd. Published 2014 by John Wiley & Sons, Ltd.

Good parenting . . .

Being overweight is bad for a child's health and can make them a target for teasing, lower their self-esteem, and make it hard for them to keep up with their friends. It may also set them up for a lifetime of feeling fat and an ongoing struggle with their weight. Good parenting is about helping your child to develop an easy approach to food so that they don't over- or undereat. Then, hopefully, food can just be one of the many things they enjoy in their life without it becoming a problem.

- **Cost:** High-fat foods could be taxed at a higher rate to deter their consumption. Fruit and vegetables could be subsidized.
- **The food industry:** Regulations could limit portion sizes and marketing could be made more transparent and honest. Vending machines for fizzy drinks and unhealthy snacks could be banned from schools.
- **Town planning:** Towns could be restructured to have cycle paths to encourage cycling rather than car use. Footpaths could be made safer and have better lighting to encourage walking. Car access to cities could be restricted or banned to encourage the use of public transport. The use of elevators could be restricted to the elderly, the disabled, and those with children, and stairs could be an available alternative.
- **Retailers:** Shops could be prevented from selling sweets and high-fat foods to children, or they could place them on high shelves where children cannot reach them.
- **Schools:** Schools could be subsidized to provide healthier meals and could place a greater emphasis on the benefits of exercise. A really interesting school-based intervention in Norway recently involved introducing exercise to many lessons other than just PE. For example, children in primary schools learned maths and literacy in the playground and ran around finding numbers to add up and collecting letters to practice their spelling. Schools could also teach children how to cook simple healthy foods and what makes a healthy meal.

Local facilities can make it easier to be active

Changing behavior

Weight gain is a simple imbalance between energy in (eating) and energy out (activity). To prevent weight gain we need to spend as much energy as we consume in our daily lives. So to prevent your child from developing a weight problem you need to make sure that eating and activity levels are at their healthiest. The tips and reality section of this book covers many ideas to encourage your child to eat more healthily (Chapter 10), to be more active (Chapter 11), to prevent your child from becoming overweight, or to help to manage their weight once they have gained weight (Chapter 12). Below are just some broad ways in which childhood obesity and later adult obesity can be prevented.

Be a good role model Up until about the age of 12 parents are by far the strongest influence on their children. After this time it might feel as if they can't bear to be near us, but in reality we are still important role models. So the most effective way to get your child to eat well and be active is through doing this yourself. So be seen to eat a healthy diet and to enjoy exercise. Prepare healthy meals, eat them in front of the children, start walking more, use the stairs not the lift, and plan for active weekends and days out. As the saying goes, "however hard you try you always end up like your mother!" So be a good role model for them to end up being like.

Say the right things   "Do as I do not as I say" is good advice to an extent as modeling healthy behaviors is the best way to get your child to be healthy. *But* at the same time saying the right things helps, and if you describe eating well and being active as positive things, your child will start to see that they are pleasures rather than chores. Don't say "Oh! Vegetables. I can't be bothered with them. I've never liked them." Say "these carrots are so crunchy," "these peas are so sweet and fresh," and "can you pass me over an apple please. I just feel like one." Likewise don't say "I'm so tired, I'm just going to crash on the sofa." Say "I'm tired. I really need some fresh air" and "after a busy week what I really fancy is a family walk." And when you eat out don't say "Pizza. This is better after all that rubbish I cook at home." Say "Oh! I could do with some salad with this pizza."

You don't need to bore your children, nag them, or patronize them (but you will do this anyway!). Just make sure that your "chat" is positive chat about all the behaviors you want them to show.

Manage their environment   You have the money and the car. You do the shopping and the cooking. You are in charge. So you can manage their environment and make it easier for them to be healthy. The government might be thinking of banning fizzy drinks in schools, asking the food industry to sell smaller portions, and making sure retailers don't put sweets on child-height shelves. But in your home you are in charge, so do the following: only bring healthy foods into the house, have a fruit bowl, take your children to cafés with healthy food on sale, buy them a skipping rope or a ball, turn the TV off, throw them out into the garden or the local park, keep regular meal times, eat at a table as a social event, make them a healthy packed lunch, and keep giving them fruit and vegetables over and over again until they concede defeat and eat them.

Many more tips are offered in the second section of this book.

Parents are in charge: manage their environment (© Adam Merrin)

How Can We Treat Obesity?

So finally, how can we treat obesity?

There are currently four key ways in which obesity can be treated: dieting, exercise, medication, and surgery. These will now be described for adults and children.

Dieting

Dieting involves eating less than you usually do and reducing your calorie intake in order to shift the energy-in/energy-out balance and lose weight. This is by far the most common approach to treating obesity and estimates suggest that up to 70 percent of women and 40 percent of men in the UK (and probably most other developed countries) have dieted at some time in their lives. There are many, many different forms of diet, which are way beyond the scope of this book. But the basic science dictates that a diet will only work if it makes you consume less energy than you use. So whether this be through eating cabbage soup for weeks on end, eating only vegetables or only protein, starving for a few days then catching up on the other days, counting calories, or having a points system, they all work on the same principle.

In general, most people who lose weight through dieting put it back on. But evidence suggests that the following might make dieting a bit more effective if you need to lose weight:

1. Don't make foods "forbidden." If you do you will end up craving them and eating even more in the longer term.
2. Make written daily plans describing what and when you are going to eat.
3. Shop with a shopping list and stick to it.
4. Only bring healthy food into the house.
5. Keep a food diary to monitor what you eat and avoid mindless eating.
6. Eat at the table not in front of the TV. This way you will be more governed by hunger and more mindful of what you are eating.
7. Work out what food means to you and when you eat too much. If you eat for emotional reasons such as when you are bored or fed up, find another way to cope with your emotions such as chatting to a friend or going for a walk.
8. Make a list of all the ways in which your weight interferes with your life.
9. Make a list of all the things that would be better about your life if you lost weight.
10. Make small sustainable changes to your diet, not huge ones; if you are not a nuts and seeds kind of person then you simply won't keep this up if you try this as a method.
11. Make changes that can be sustained forever, not just a few weeks. Losing weight then putting it back on is demoralizing and bad for your health.
12. Eat three meals a day at a specified time. Don't snack. If you know what and when you are going to eat next, it will make feeling hungry between meals more manageable.
13. Always eat breakfast.

For children, however, things are a bit different. The last thing you want to do with children is to make food into an issue. If your child is a bit over-weight using the charts in Chapter 5, encourage them to be more active and control the kinds of foods available to them (see Chapter 12). But don't put them on a diet. In fact don't even mention dieting as the chances are they will suddenly shoot up and lose the weight. You don't want to risk the possibility of them becoming obsessed with food, and there is so much evidence that the more you try to avoid foods the more preoccupied with them you become.

But if your child is obese using these charts, then it is time to take action. First start by encouraging them to be more active and controlling the kinds of foods they have access to (Chapters 11 and 12). Try to always eat at the table, not in front of the TV, discourage snacking, always give them breakfast, and make sure you all have three meals a day. And be a good role model by eating healthily and being active. Give this time and see what happens. Then start to be more proactive in terms of the rest of the suggestions in the list above. But be careful. If you make food forbidden, or make your child feel ugly, self-conscious, and different, the chances are they will eat even more, then feel guilty, and then eat even more to cope with the guilt. Chapter 12 offers tips for a child who eats too much and Chapter 11 describes ways to help them become more active.

Exercise

Exercise is great for health regardless of weight. But if you or your child are overweight or obese then being more active will help you to lose weight and keep it off. Chapter 11 offers tips for becoming more active as a family. But in general, the recommendations are the same as for preventing obesity: be a good role model, say the right things, and manage your child's environment.

Have active days out

Medication

If both dietary and exercise treatments have failed, then an obese individual may turn to drugs; as Hirsch said in 1998, "Who would not rejoice to find a magic bullet that we could fire into obese people to make them permanently slim and healthy?" (47). Doctors have been offering weight-loss drugs for many years and in the past often used to prescribe amphetamines (known commonly as speed), a practice which was stopped due to the drug's addictive qualities. Nowadays, drug therapy is only legally available to patients in the UK with a BMI of 30 or more, and government bodies have become increasingly restrictive on the use of anti-obesity drugs.

There are currently two groups of anti-obesity drugs available, which are offered in conjunction with dietary and exercise programs. Those in the first group suppress appetite. Although there is some evidence for the effectiveness of these drugs, they can also be accompanied by side-effects such as nausea, dry mouth, and constipation. Recently all of these drugs have been removed from the market due to the risk of heart attacks and lowered mood.

The second group of drugs, currently in use, reduce fat absorption. Orlistat is one of these and can cause weight loss in obese subjects. It is, however, accompanied by a range of unpleasant side-effects, including liquid stools, an urgent need to go to the toilet, and anal leakage, which are particularly apparent following a high-fat meal. At present there is an over-the-counter version of Orlistat called "Ali" which is a lower dose than that prescribed by the doctor but which has a similar effect. My researchers and I have carried out studies in this area which suggest that when Orlistat works, it does so by making obese people realize that their weight is caused by what they eat rather than their biological makeup, as simply seeing the fat in their diet come out in such an unpleasant way helps them make the link between fat eaten and fat stored in the body. They then change their diet (48). An easier way would be to simply encourage overweight and obese people to recognize the role of diet in their weight problem without having to resort to such an unpleasant drug.

At present Orlistat is not licensed for use in children although there are ongoing studies exploring whether or not it could be used alongside dietary advice.

Surgery

The final approach to treating obesity is surgery. This has gained a huge amount of media attention over the past few years and generated responses varying from "at last something that works" to "it's cheating. They have made themselves fat and don't deserve the expense." In the UK, US, and across most European countries surgery is available for those with a BMI greater than 40, or 35 if they have other health problems such as diabetes or hypertension. Although there are 21 different surgical procedures for obesity the two most popular are the gastric bypass and gastric banding. The gastric bypass promotes weight loss in two ways. First it reduces the amount of food that can be eaten, as large quantities of food cause discomfort, and second it reduces how much food is absorbed once it has been eaten. The gastric bypass is irreversible except under extreme circumstances. In contrast, gastric banding can be reversed more easily and involves the use of a band to create a small pouch of stomach. This procedure works simply by restricting food intake, as once the pouch is full any further food induces vomiting.

Researchers in Sweden carried out the large-scale Swedish Obese Subjects (SOS) study which explored nearly 1,000 matched pairs of patients who received either surgery or conventional treatment for their obesity (49). The results indicated that surgery can be effective for both weight loss and maintenance and brings with it a reduction in the risk factors for heart disease. It is not all good news, however, as some individuals who have surgery do not lose as much weight as expected or show weight regain. They may also lose weight too quickly and become malnourished. In addition, some are left with large amounts of unsightly excess skin which is difficult to manage and requires further expensive plastic surgery.

My researchers and I have carried out studies exploring the psychological effects of obesity surgery and showed that not only does weight loss cause improved self-esteem and confidence, which you would expect from any method that worked, but also people felt less hungry, less preoccupied with food, and more in control of their eating behavior. I have called this "the paradox of control" as by taking away control from the individual, they paradoxically feel more in control. I see this as a bit like having an internal nanny state or bossy mother sitting in your stomach restricting what you can eat: because you can't eat as much as you used to, the decisions have been made for you, which can be quite liberating in a world full of food (50).

Some clinicians have called for the use of obesity surgery with adolescents, arguing that it is best to treat obesity as early as possible to prevent the onset of obesity-related conditions. This is a controversial move as most operations are irreversible. Currently in the UK there are only a few centers that offer surgery to children and the criteria are very strict. In particular,

Take home points

- Government approaches to obesity prevention involve changing the environment through advertising laws, introducing taxes on high-fat foods, removing vending machines from schools, and making school dinners healthier.
- Prevention can also occur at home.
- Home prevention involves managing your child's environment by buying and cooking healthy food, being a good role model, and saying the right things about food.
- The most common form of obesity treatment is dieting, which may cause weight loss but can also cause weight gain in the longer term.
- Healthier dieting involves not having forbidden foods, making clear plans, buying and cooking healthy food, eating mindfully at the table and not on the go or in front of the TV, and making small sustainable changes to your diet.
- Exercise can also help weight loss and keeping this weight off.
- Some people turn to medication or surgery but this is very rare for children.

it is only offered for a child with a BMI of 50 or above (or 40 if they have a serious health condition) and they have to be considered physically mature (about 13 for girls and 15 for boys). Private hospitals elsewhere in the world, however, are not as strict, and children with less severe obesity have been given surgery in other countries.

In Summary

Over the past 30 years there has been a dramatic increase in the numbers of adults and children who are obese or overweight. The key causes of this are an obesogenic environment which makes it easier to gain weight, and two key behaviors: eating too much and not being active enough. Obesity is therefore the product of a simple energy-in/energy-out balance, and prevention and treatments focus on changing this balance. Public health approaches to prevention mainly target the environment through addressing factors such as food advertising, cost, the food industry, retailers, town planning, or schools. This approach aims to make it easier to stay healthy by making the environment less obesogenic. Other approaches focus directly on behavior and encourage healthier lifestyles. As a parent the best approach to preventing obesity in your children is threefold: (i) be a good role model and be seen to eat well and to be active; (ii) say the right things about healthy food and exercise, making them fun and "normal" in the family; (iii) manage your child's environment by buying in healthy foods, turning off the TV, and encouraging them to play by being as active as possible. In terms of treatments, these also tackle behavior. The most common approaches are dieting and exercise, although many adults are now turning to medication or surgery. These may be used for children in extreme cases but this is still rare. Prevention, however, is by far the more effective approach. It is more effective than any treatment. So, if possible, help prevent your child from becoming overweight in the first place.

7

Eating disorders
Prevalence, consequences, and causes

There are many different eating disorders, including anorexia nervosa (AN) (excessive weight loss), bulimia nervosa (BN) (bingeing and purging), binge eating disorder (BED) (binge eating but without purging), orthorexia (excessive concern about healthy eating), and eating disorder not otherwise specified (EDNOS) (a general term for other forms of eating disorders which don't quite fulfill the criteria for other problems). This chapter will focus on AN and BN as they tend to be the most well-known forms of eating disorders and often generate the most concern in parents. Many of their characteristics, however, are also relevant to other forms of eating disorders. How eating disorders can be prevented and possible treatments are described in the next chapter (Chapter 8). This chapter will explore the following:

- What are AN and BN?
- How common are they?
- What do people with AN and BN do?
- What are the consequences of AN and BN?
- What are their causes?

The Good Parenting Food Guide: Managing What Children Eat without Making Food a Problem, First Edition. Jane Ogden.

Good parenting . . .

Having a child with an eating disorder is extremely upsetting for parents as they can feel powerless and frightened about the future. They may also worry about what they have done wrong and sometimes parents can turn against each other in their struggle to make sense of what has happened. Having an eating disorder is also extremely distressing for the child and can color all aspects of their life including their school work, friends, and relationship with their family. Good parenting is about finding ways to prevent an eating disorder from developing in the first place, noticing any early signs, and creating a home environment in which their children can find outlets for their problems other than food.

Anorexia Nervosa (AN)

What is AN?

A disorder involving severe emaciation and loss of periods (amenorrhea) was first described by Lasègue as "l'anorexie hystérique" in 1873 and by Gull in 1874 as "Anorexia Nervosa," meaning "nervous loss of appetite." These early descriptions actually misname the problem as most people with AN do feel hungry – they just manage not to eat. Currently, the definition most frequently used states that AN involves the following factors:

- Refusal to maintain body weight at or above a minimally normal weight for age and height (e.g. weight loss leading to maintenance of body weight less than 85 percent of that expected, or failure to make expected weight gain during periods of growth, leading to body weight less than 85 percent of that expected). A BMI of 18 is the usual cut-off.
- Intense fear of gaining weight or becoming fat even though underweight.
- Disturbance in the way in which body weight or shape is experienced, a central role for body weight or shape in self-evaluation, or denial of the current low body weight.
- Missing at least three consecutive menstrual cycles (for girls post-puberty or women).

There are generally two types of AN: restricting anorexia, which involves food restriction and no episodes of bingeing; and purging and binge eating anorexia, which involves both food restriction and episodes of bingeing or purging through self-induced vomiting or the misuse of laxatives, diuretics, or enemas.

How common is AN?

In the Western world about 1 percent of women develop AN, and although this rate increased between 1950 and the mid-1980s it has stabilized in recent years. The majority of people with AN are female. The male to female ratio is 1:10, although there has been an increase in men with AN in vulnerable groups such as models, dancers, and jockeys, who are required to have a lower body weight. The average age of onset is about 17 years, although there is some evidence that this is getting earlier and some hospitals now have patients as young as 8. At such an early age, however, it is hard to see whether the child has AN or another form of "feeding disorder" such as "selective eating," "food phobias," or "food refusal." AN can also start in middle age or even older. It is estimated that 1 percent of all cases start after the age of 40, and several new cases have been recognized in women in their seventies.

What do people with AN do?

All people with AN restrict their food intake. Most are extremely knowledgeable about the nutritional content of food, and count every calorie. When they do eat they tend to eat small meals predominantly made up of fruit and vegetables. They eat very slowly, sometimes cutting the food into small pieces. They avoid all fatty foods and often drink coffee and fizzy drinks, chew gum, or smoke, to minimize their hunger. The diet of people with AN is often repetitive and ritualized and they eat from a very limited repertoire. Many cook elaborate meals for others and buy and read magazines and books containing recipes and pictures of food. Some refuse to swallow their food and chew it and then spit it out. Others will binge on large quantities of food and then purge by using laxatives or diuretics or making themselves sick. Some also fidget when sitting, or march backwards and forwards as a means to burn up calories. Some sufferers of anorexia also hoard food.

Good descriptions of what anorexics actually do can be found in accounts from survivors of anorexia and semi-autobiographical novels.

For example, one woman described how "I was eating fruit and dry crispbreads, lettuce and celery and a very little lean meat. My diet was unvaried. Every day had to be the same. I panicked if the shop did not have exactly the brand of crispbread I wanted, I panicked if I could not eat, ritually, at the same time" (17). Shute's novel *Life-size* (51) described in detail an anorexic's eating:

> peas were good because you could eat them one by one, spearing each on a single tine. Brussels sprouts were good, because you could unwrap them leaf by leaf and make them last forever. Corn could be nibbled, a few kernels at a time . . . Potatoes were evil. I would never eat one, no matter what . . .

Shute also provided insights into the other main aspect of anorexia, namely feeling fat. She wrote:

> I knew I still had much to lose. There was still fat on my stomach, a handful above the navel and a roll below. I pinched it hard several times an hour to remind myself that it was there, that nothing mattered more than getting rid of it . . . one day I will be thin enough. Just the bones, no disfiguring flesh, just the pure, clear shape of me.

What are the consequences of AN?

The physical and psychological problems associated with anorexia nervosa are as follows:

Death: A girl with AN is twice as likely to die from her condition compared to those with any other psychological problem. The most common causes of death are suicide, infection, digestive problems, and heart failure caused by malnutrition. In fact a person with AN is 58 times more likely to commit suicide than someone without AN. It is also estimated that a patient diagnosed with AN aged 15 can be predicted to live for 25 years less than someone without AN (52). AN is therefore a very serious life-threatening condition.

Skeleton and teeth: Adolescence is the key time for the development of bones, and malnutrition causes poor bone growth and decreased bone density. If anorexia develops at this time, the sufferer may be left with the irreversible problems of stunted growth. It can also lead to osteoporosis, and there is some evidence that this is worse in male sufferers than in female sufferers. Teeth are also affected by anorexia, particularly if the sufferer vomits regularly, as this causes erosion of the tooth enamel, making the teeth vulnerable to caries. Tooth erosion is sometimes the symptom by which persistent vomiting is recognized by health professionals.

Reproductive function: Starvation directly affects menstrual functioning, and the absence of menstrual periods is a key way to diagnose AN. In fact AN has been reported as the cause of infertility in about 16 percent of women attending fertility clinics. Those women who do become pregnant while anorexic are more likely to have premature or small babies who may have complications such as respiratory distress and jaundice. For the majority of people with AN, periods restart once weight has been regained.

The cardiovascular and nervous systems: Many deaths from anorexia are caused by heart attacks, possibly due to low levels of calcium or magnesium or a collapse of the mitral valve in the heart. Anorexia is also associated with changes in the nervous system which may cause problems such as poor attention, memory loss, a poor sense of space, and slower learning.

Depression: Just under half of patients with AN also suffer from depression, which tends to be higher among those anorexics who binge or purge.

Anxiety disorders: A majority of people with AN also suffer from anxiety-related disorders such as social phobia and obsessive compulsive behaviors.

AN is therefore a serious life-threatening condition with a high mortality rate. It is also associated with problems with the cardiovascular and nervous systems due to malnutrition, and is linked with depression and anxiety.

Bulimia Nervosa (BN)

What is BN?

The term "bulimia nervosa" was first used by Gerald Russell in 1979 to describe a version of anorexia nervosa in 30 of his patients (53). A more recent description of BN is as follows:

- Recurrent episodes of binge eating. An episode of binge eating involves both (1) eating in a discrete period of time (e.g. in any two-hour period) an amount of food that is definitely larger than most people would eat in a similar period of time (taking into account time since last meal and social context in which eating occurred), and (2) a sense of lack of control over eating during the episode (e.g. a feeling that one can't stop eating or control what or how much one is eating).

- Recurrent use of inappropriate compensatory behavior to avoid weight gain, e.g. self-induced vomiting, laxative use.
- A minimum average of two episodes of binge eating and two inappropriate compensatory behaviors a week for at least three months.
- Self-evaluation which is overly based upon body shape and weight.
- The disturbance not occurring exclusively during episodes of anorexia nervosa.

BN can be divided into the purging type (those who binge and purge using vomiting and/or laxatives) and the non-purging type (those who binge only). The non-purging type of patients mostly use excessive exercise or dieting as a means to compensate for food intake.

How common is BN?

About 2 percent of women in the Western world develop BN, although this number is difficult to estimate as many people with BN never come into contact with health professionals. It is therefore about twice as common as AN. The majority of sufferers are women (the male to female ratio is 1:10) and the average age of onset is about 18 years (slightly older than AN). It was very rare prior to 1979 but its incidence has dramatically increased since this time. As with AN, however, the rate has stabilized in recent years.

What do people with BN do?

People with BN are usually within the normal weight range and maintain this weight through the processes of bingeing and purging. Bingeing involves eating a large amount of food in a discrete amount of time; foods eaten include sweet high-fat foods such as ice cream, doughnuts, pudding, chocolate, biscuits, and cakes. Other foods eaten include breads and pasta, cheeses, meats, and snack foods such as peanuts and crisps. One study measured the food intake of a group of normal-weight women with bulimia and reported an average intake of 7,101 kcals during a bingeing episode, compared to a daily intake of 1,844 kcals by normal-weight healthy women. Such binges are accompanied by feelings of loss of control, are usually carried out in secret, involve very quick eating, and consist mainly of the foods that the patient is attempting to avoid in order to lose weight. The consequences of a binge are described by Shute (51): "my stomach, pressing painfully in all directions, could hold no more. I needed to collapse. Belching in rancid, vomity bursts, oozing oil from my pores, heavy and numb with self hatred ... Avoiding the mirrors I pulled off my clothes, releasing an unrecognisable belly; my waistband left a vicious red stripe, but I only looked once."

Sufferers of BN also engage in compensatory behavior as a means to manage any weight gain caused by the binges. The most common form is self-induced vomiting, which usually occurs at the end of a binge but also after episodes of normal eating. One study reported that three-quarters of their bulimic sample vomited at least once a day and nearly half vomited twice a day. This is usually achieved through the gag reflex using fingers, although many bulimics learn to vomit spontaneously. Vomiting is accompanied by feelings of self-disgust and loathing, is almost always secret, and may go undetected for years. Vomiting also provides a great sense of relief from the sense of distension caused by overeating and the fear of weight gain. It can therefore become habit-forming and encourages further overeating and further vomiting. In fact, although binge eating may start off as the primary behavior which causes vomiting, it has been argued that over time vomiting can start to drive bingeing.

Bulimics also use laxatives and diuretics as a means to compensate for bingeing. This behavior can also become habit-forming, particularly if the individual develops tolerance to the substances used and needs to increase their intake to maintain their effectiveness.

What are the consequences of BN?

Bulimia nervosa is associated with a range of physical and psychological problems. Some of these are clearly consequences of the bulimia. For others it is unclear whether they are causes, consequences, or just co-occur. Long-term follow-ups of bulimics indicate that about 70 percent recover, 10 percent stay fully symptomatic, and the remaining 20 percent show great variability in their symptoms. The most common consequences are as follows:

Death: The mortality rate for bulimia is much lower than for anorexia and is estimated at between 1 and 3 percent. Those who do die appear to have received a diagnosis of anorexia at some time in their history, and the most common cause of death is suicide. Of Russell's original patients, 11 out of the 30 had made a suicide attempt. Larger studies set the rate at about 16 percent and actual suicide rates are much higher than in the normal healthy population (54).

Cardiovascular problems: Due to nutritional deficits and the disturbance of bodily fluids caused by laxative and diuretic abuse, bulimics show cardiovascular problems such as palpitations, irregular and missed heartbeats, low blood pressure, and sometimes heart failure.

Digestive problems: Due to the movement of stomach acid caused by the binge/purge cycle bulimics also suffer from digestive problems including dyspepsia, constipation, diarrhea, and pancreatitis, they may have sore throats, and they often have dental caries and abscesses. They show muscle cramps and have skin problems such as dry flaky skin and calluses on the backs of their hands and fingers from induced vomiting.

Neurotic symptoms: Bulimia is also associated with neurotic symptoms such as pathological guilt, worrying, poor concentration, obsessional ideas, rumination, nervous tension, hopelessness, and inefficient thinking.

Depression: Many people with BN also experience depression, and the lifetime rate of major depression among patients with bulimia has been reported to range from 36 percent to 70 percent. Studies also show that at the time of presentation for treatment between one-third and one-half of patients are clinically depressed.

Anxiety: The majority of bulimic patients also report anxiety symptoms including feeling anxious about eating in public and getting undressed in a communal area, and experiencing anxiety-related symptoms when thinking about food, weight, or shape.

Addictions: Bulimia is also associated with addictive behaviors such as alcohol and substance abuse. In addition, those with bulimia may also suffer from conduct disorder and a tendency to steal. It has been suggested that bulimia is related to poor impulse control, which may explain some of the behaviors associated with this condition.

BN is therefore a serious condition associated with a range of physical and health problems. Suicide rates are high in this patient group but it is not as life-threatening as AN and patients can continue with BN for many years without coming into contact with the health care system.

What Causes Eating Disorders?

Since the increased interest in both AN and BN and other related eating disorders researchers have developed many theories to explain their cause. These theories tend to fall into different perspectives, such as a cognitive behavioral approach with a focus on learning and reinforcement, a family systems approach with a focus on family dynamics, or a social cultural approach which focuses on the role of the media and the meanings of food and size. In general, however, no one theory seems to provide the perfect answer and each has its problems. I have therefore decided to describe the key factors that cut across these different approaches and which best help us to understand why one person may develop an eating disorder. These can be considered contributory factors rather than causes *per se* as they each increase the likelihood that someone will develop an eating disorder but are not full explanations on their own.

Body dissatisfaction

Body dissatisfaction comes in many forms and is increasingly common among men and women, girls and boys. Some people believe their body to be larger than it really is, which can be measured using distorting mirrors or by asking people to adjust the distance between two light beams to match the width of different aspects of their body. Some people also express body dissatisfaction in terms of a gap between how they perceive themselves to be and how they would like to be. This research has tended to use whole-body silhouette pictures of varying sizes and the subject is asked to state which one is closest to how they look now and which one best illustrates how they would like to look (see Figure 7.1).

Research shows that many people also have negative feelings about their body size and shape. This is assessed using questions such as "Do you worry about parts of your body being too big?" "Do you worry about your thighs spreading out when you sit down?" and "Does being with thin women make you feel conscious of your weight?"

In general, the research indicates that people with eating disorders show greater distortion of their body size than those without eating disorders but that the vast majority of women, with or without an eating disorder, think that they are fatter than they actually are. It has also consistently been shown that most girls and women would like to be thinner than they are

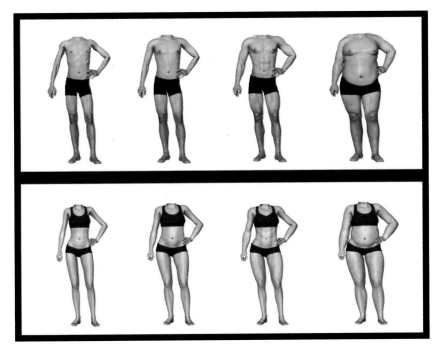

Figure 7.1   Measuring body dissatisfaction
Source: Ara Cho and Jang-Han Lee. 2013. Body dissatisfaction levels and gender differences in attentional biases toward idealized bodies. *Body Image*, 10(1), 95–102. http://dx.doi.org/10.1016/j.bodyim.2012.09.005. (http://www.sciencedirect.com/science/article/pii/S1740144512001295). Reproduced with permission of Elsevier.

and most males would like to be either the same size or larger. In particular, women would prefer their chests to be larger and their legs, stomachs, bottoms, and overall body shape to be smaller, and show greater dissatisfaction than men. Such gender differences are apparent in children as young as 9 years. Many boys and men, however, are also dissatisfied with their bodies and would prefer their arms, chests, and shoulders to be larger and their stomachs and overall body to be smaller.

Body dissatisfaction has been linked to eating disorders as it may lead to dieting and food restriction which in turn can lead to more extreme forms of eating-related problems.

The media

The most commonly held belief is that body dissatisfaction is a response to the use of images of thin women in the media. Magazines, newspapers, television, films, and even novels predominantly use images of thin women. These women may be advertising body-size-related items such as food and clothes or neutral items such as vacuum cleaners and wallpaper, but they are always thin. Alternatively, they may be characters in a story or simply passers-by to illustrate the real world, but this real world is always thin.

Media images can make children dissatisfied with how they look

Whatever their role and wherever they appear, women and men used by the media are generally thin, and we are therefore led to believe that thinness is not only the desired norm but also *the* norm. When, on those rare occasions, a fatter woman appears, she is usually there making a statement about being fat (fat comedians make jokes about chocolate cake and fat actresses are either evil or unhappy), not simply as a normal woman. In the past decade or so, men with the "perfect" body have also increasingly been used to sell products, whether it be fizzy drinks being drunk by half-naked window cleaners at 11 o'clock, jeans which need to be removed and shrunk in a washing machine, or deodorant.

Some research has directly explored the association between the media and body dissatisfaction. For example, studies show that young girls who spend more time reading popular magazines and watching television show higher levels of body dissatisfaction (55). Studies have also shown that asking women to examine images of thin women from magazines for just a few minutes in the laboratory can make them feel more dissatisfied with the way they look (56). Imagine what long-term exposure over many years could do!

My colleagues and I have carried out studies to teach women to become more critical of the images in magazines by highlighting techniques such as airbrushing, lighting, and makeup (57). This approach could easily be used with children to make them less vulnerable to the images they see around them. Images used by the media can therefore make people dissatisfied with how they look, which in turn may lead to dieting and subsequent eating disorders.

Dieting

Body dissatisfaction often leads to dieting, and studies indicate that up to 70 percent of women have dieted at some time in their lives as a means to lose weight and change their body shape. At times this can be healthy and lead to weight loss in those who are obese or overweight. For many dieters, however, although dieting may result in brief episodes of undereating and weight loss, these are mostly followed by overeating and weight regain.

Most dieting is characterized by trying not to eat as much food or the kinds of food that people still really want to eat. Vegetarians may be able to avoid meat because they just don't want to eat it. But dieters are trying to avoid food they still want to eat. This leads to a state of denial which is pretty much impossible to sustain. Furthermore, by trying not to eat foods they want to eat, these foods become more forbidden and therefore even more desirable than before. And eventually dieters give in and overeat. We call this the "what the hell effect" as after one biscuit people think "what the hell" and eat the whole packet, which is very similar to how smokers feel when they are trying to give up smoking or alcoholics on the wagon feel after their first slip back down the slippery slope.

An American researcher called Wegner carried out an interesting study which I think helps to explain this behavior. It is called the white bear study and involved telling half a group of people *never* to think about a white bear. He then told the other half to think about a white bear whenever they wanted to, and gave them all a bell to ring if ever they thought of a white bear. Wegner found that those who had been told *never* to think about a white bear rang their bell all the time (58). For dieters, they think "I mustn't eat chips," "I must eat less," "I mustn't have those biscuits," and then, as in the white bear study, chips and biscuits are all they can think about. And eventually they give in and eat even more chips and biscuits than if they hadn't been trying to avoid them in the first place.

We want what we can't have (© Adam Merrin)

Many people with eating disorders have dieted first as a means to change their body size and weight. This in turn can create a preoccupation with food and a tendency to fluctuate between undereating and overeating. For a minority this can lead to an eating disorder such as anorexia or bulimia nervosa.

Genetics

Eating disorders appear to run in families. For example, female relatives of patients with AN are 10 times more likely to develop an eating disorder than a population unrelated to someone with AN. Similarly, BN is also more common in families of patients with BN. Interestingly, the type of eating disorder appears to be specific, with anorexia being more common in families of anorexics and bulimia being more common in families of bulimics.

Clustering within families suggests a role for genetics but cannot rule out the impact of a shared environment. Researchers have therefore carried out twin studies using identical and non-identical twins. In general, the twin data provide some support for a genetic influence in anorexia, particularly restricting anorexia, but a much weaker role, if any, in the development of bulimia. How a genetic predisposition expresses itself remains unclear. Some researchers have pointed to the role of obsessive compulsive disorder, perfectionism, and body dissatisfaction as risk factors. This suggests that the genetic predisposition expresses itself in a greater tendency towards these factors, which then trigger anorexia.

The meaning of symptoms

Refusing to eat, bingeing, and weight loss play a strong role in the life of a person with an eating disorder, and some researchers have focused on the meaning of these symptoms, with a particular emphasis on control. In particular it has been argued that if an individual feels out of control of other aspects of their life such as their parents, friendships, school work, or future, food can offer them one area in which they can be in charge. Refusing food therefore means "This is an area in which I am in control." Furthermore, becoming very thin and losing weight is a very public statement which will be noticed, commented on, and reacted to by those around the person concerned. Losing weight therefore means "I am only a little child, I cannot live by myself, I have to be looked after." From this perspective an eating disorder can be seen as a way to communicate to the outside world "I am in control but I need help." Therefore in the same way that we can read a book, a song, or even "read" what someone is wearing, symptoms can be read and in general the symptoms of an eating disorder mean that something is wrong and that the person would like some help.

The mother–daughter relationship

Much research in this area focuses on the role of childhood and particularly the mother–daughter relationship. Many disorders, such as anxiety, depression, or issues of anger management, seem to emerge out of families where there are high levels of conflict and neglect. Eating disorders seem to emerge from the opposite kinds of families, with mothers who have anticipated their child's every need and have understood when the child was hungry, thirsty, or tired. When children are brought up by apparently "perfect" mothers they may feel ineffectual and grow up unable to identify and understand their own needs. They then develop an eating disorder as a means to regain control and assert themselves over their mother.

Role models

Eating disorders may run in families in part due to genetics. But children also learn how to behave from their parents and it is clear that mothers (in particular) who are critical of their own bodies and have their own issues with food can communicate these problems to their children. This in turn can make it seem normal and acceptable to have low body esteem and can also normalize problematic attitudes and behaviors around food.

Family dynamics

Families are said to exist in homeostasis. This means that like a central heating system they maintain the status quo by constantly making small adjustments. For example, if one parent is particularly argumentative the other may become very passive to keep the family together. Similarly if one parent becomes very absent the family will shift roles to adjust to this change. Sometimes in families a child develops an eating disorder to compensate for another change that has happened, most often a shift in the relationship between the parents. Therefore if the parents' marriage starts to fall apart, a child may develop an eating disorder as a means to bring them back together again. This is not a conscious decision but is driven by the need for a sense of equilibrium and normality.

Eating disorders can also emerge when boundaries in the family are problematic. Common problems in families with a child with an eating disorder are:

- **Enmeshment:** an extreme form of over-involvement and intimacy, i.e. living your life through your child
- **Over-protectiveness:** an extreme level of concern and fear of the child moving away from the family
- **Rigidity:** a determination to maintain the status quo whatever the consequences
- **A lack of conflict resolution:** families who avoid conflict or are in a permanent state of chronic conflict may end up with a child with an eating disorder

Reinforcement

Any behavior that receives attention, even negative attention, can be reinforced, making it more likely to happen again. This is why the most powerful thing you can do to a child's behavior is ignore it. In terms of AN, it is argued the individual reduces their food intake as a means to lose weight due to the social pressure to be thin and a general sense of dissatisfaction with their life. This behavior is then reinforced in a multitude of ways, such as approval from others – "you look well" – *and* disapproval from others – "you look too thin," "you haven't finished your meal," "you need to eat more." Having an empty stomach may also be reinforcing as it can be experienced as pleasurable, and not eating may generate a feeling of being in control. Reinforcing food avoidance and weight loss sets the individual off into a downward spiral, encouraging their behavior, as although it seems dysfunctional from the outside, for them it is working as they are getting attention from others and feeling more in control of their life.

In terms of BN, a similar pattern emerges, with both weight loss and feeling empty being reinforced. People with BN may also find the sensation of purging reinforcing as it provides relief from the feeling of extreme fullness they have after a binge.

Perfectionism

Perfectionism is very closely related to anxiety and seems to be on the increase according to the university counselors who see all our struggling students. Many people with eating disorders tend to show a perfectionistic tendency, reflecting a desire for total control and total success. Accordingly, they don't just want to be good at school, but the best. They also want to win their races on sports days and get the highest marks in their music exams. If they become dissatisfied with how they look or their life in general, they may start to diet as a means to lose weight. They will then be driven to be the "best dieter" and to be "the most in control of their eating" as they apply their perfectionism to this new set of targets.

Faulty thinking

Many people with eating disorders show faulty thinking or "cognitive dysfunctions" as they process information in ways that can seem irrational to others. These faulty thoughts help the development of an eating disorder as the person can no longer see anything wrong with their behavior and searches out evidence to justify how they are behaving. Common forms of faulty thinking are:

- **Focusing on selected evidence**, such as "I am very special if I am thin" and "the only way I can be in control is through eating."
- **Black and white thinking**, which involves thinking in terms of extremes, such as "if I am not in complete control I will lose all control" and "if I put on one pound I will become fat."
- **Over-generalization**, which involves drawing conclusions from single events and then generalizing to all others, such as "I failed last night so I will fail today as well."
- **Magnification**, which involves exaggeration, such as "gaining two pounds will push me over the brink."
- **Superstitious thinking**, which involves making connections between unconnected things, such as "if I eat this it will be converted into fat immediately."
- **Personalization**, which involves making sense of events in a self-centered fashion, such as "they were laughing, they must be laughing at me."

The food restriction shown by a person with an eating disorder is therefore reinforced through pressures to be thin and the praise or concern that this brings. The high value placed on thinness and the fear of becoming fat are established and perpetuated through their faulty thinking, which gets increasingly well established and is challenged less and less as they become more isolated from people around them.

A significant event as a trigger

Sometimes, eating disorders can be triggered by life events. The three most commonly studied life events are childhood sexual abuse, parental loss, and transition between schools or leaving home.

Childhood sexual abuse   Many patients with eating disorders disclose sexual abuse during the treatment process, and research indicates that about 30 percent of individuals with an eating disorder have been sexually abused in childhood. Those in treatment, however, are more likely to disclose abuse as they are having treatment. It is therefore generally believed that this rate of abuse is similar to that found in women without eating disorders, but lower than that reported by other psychiatric patients. This literature was reviewed and the authors concluded that "child sexual abuse is neither necessary nor sufficient for the development of an eating disorder," but suggested that childhood sexual abuse is "best considered a risk factor" (59).

The picture for men, however, may be different. For example, one study explored the history of childhood sexual abuse in 193 gay and bisexual men who were white, black, or Latino, and also assessed the presence or absence of an eating disorder (60). The results showed that the rate of childhood sexual abuse was far higher in those with many different types of eating disorder (e.g. subclinical bulimia, AN, or BN) and that this relationship persisted even when depression and/or a substance use disorder were controlled for. Accordingly, the authors argue that eating disorders may be a potential mechanism used by gay or bisexual men to cope with abuse in their childhood.

Parental loss   Studies show no simple association between parental separation or death of a parent and the development of an eating disorder. If the meaning of loss is expanded to include parental separation, death of a parent, death of a close family member, or being sent to boarding school, then there does seem to be a link with the development of both AN and BN. The possible mechanism for this may be unresolved grief, but to date this has not been tested.

Transitional period   Eating disorders often seem to start following a period of transition, whether it be from primary to secondary school, leaving school to go to university, or leaving home. Such times are highly stressful and can create feelings of loss and an identity crisis as people struggle to decide who they want to be. If the individual turns to food as a means for self-control and if this is reinforced in the ways described above, then the development of an eating problem may help to "solve" some of the problems they are feeling by creating a new identity, giving them a focus, and enabling them to feel in control of at least one area of their life.

Control

One issue that seems central to many of the factors described above is that of control. For example, children who have over-protective parents or an enmeshed relationship with their mother might feel out of control. Further, those who are dissatisfied with their bodies and have a history of failed attempts at dieting may also feel that their lives are out of their control. Furthermore, at times of transition or after a life event, life can feel uncontrollable for everyone. Eating disorders are often therefore seen as an attempt to regain some control over an apparently out of control existence. So, even though a person may not be able to control their parents' breakup, or what happens to them after they have left home, or gone to university, or their body size, *at least* they can feel able to control how much food they eat. And although to others a person with an eating disorder may seem out of control, from their own perspective they have settled on something that makes their life feel less frightening and chaotic and more manageable.

There is therefore a wide range of factors that contribute to the development of an eating disorder, ranging from genetics, to role models, family dynamics, faulty thinking, and issues of control. None of these provides a complete explanation and none can be seen as a cause on its own. For example, although many people feel that the media are to blame and that eating disorders are driven by body dissatisfaction and dieting, the majority of girls, in particular, show body dissatisfaction but only a small minority develop an eating disorder. In addition, although AN seems to have a genetic basis, this is by no means clear-cut, and just because a mother has had an eating disorder does not mean that her daughter will as well. Furthermore, even though some kinds of family dynamics seem to explain why some children develop an eating problem, many people who have eating disorders come from very different types of families. So eating disorders remain difficult to predict and are certainly not the inevitable consequence of a certain childhood or a specific society. The best we have is some idea of the kinds of factors that may make an eating disorder more likely.

In Summary

Although there are several different forms of eating disorder this chapter has focused on AN and BN as they are the ones parents are most concerned about. In addition, many of their characteristics, such as food avoidance, bingeing, purging, low self-esteem, and body dissatisfaction, are also part of other diagnoses. AN and BN only affect about 1–2 percent of the female population in the Western world but they are serious conditions and linked with a number of physical and psychological problems including cardiovascular disease, suicide, depression, and anxiety. There are many possible factors which contribute to the development of eating disorders, including perfectionism, family dynamics, reinforcement, body dissatisfaction, and

Take home points

- AN and BN are quite rare and affect about 1–2 percent of the female population in the Western world.
- AN has the highest mortality rate of any psychological problem and is also linked with problems of the heart, bones, and teeth, reproduction, and depression.
- BN is linked with suicide as well as addictions, depression and anxiety, and problems with the heart and digestive system.
- The causes of AN and BN are complex.
- Possible risk factors are body dissatisfaction and dieting.
- AN and BN are also associated with genetics, issues of control, family dynamics, perfectionism, faulty thinking, and using symptoms to express that something is wrong.

dieting, but central to many of these is the issue of control, with people turning to food as a means to control their lives. The next chapter will describe several ways to prevent the development of an eating disorder and outline the kinds of treatments available. Specific tips for managing a child who is undereating are described in Chapter 13, and tips for helping a child who feels fat are given in Chapter 14.

8

Eating disorders
Prevention and treatments

The previous chapter described the two eating disorders anorexia nervosa (AN) and bulimia nervosa (BN) in terms of their definitions, how common they are, what people with these conditions do, and their possible causes. This chapter will explore the following:

- How can eating disorders be prevented?
- What treatments are available?

These issues are relevant to all diagnoses of eating disorders as they all involve attempts at food restriction, low body esteem, and several include episodes of bingeing and/or purging.

How Can We Prevent Eating Disorders?

Given that there are many different factors that may contribute to the development of an eating disorder, preventing an eating disorder is more difficult than preventing obesity. Here are some simple ways, however, to minimize the risks. The chapters in the second half of this book cover some of these in greater detail (in particular, see Chapter 13 for managing a child who is undereating and Chapter 14 for a child who thinks they are fat).

The Good Parenting Food Guide: Managing What Children Eat without Making Food a Problem, First Edition. Jane Ogden.
© 2014 John Wiley & Sons, Ltd. Published 2014 by John Wiley & Sons, Ltd.

Good parenting . . .

Eating disorders seem irrational and self-destructive from the outside. But to the person with an eating disorder their behavior makes perfect sense as it helps them to manage their life. Good parenting is about being a good role model for body confidence and eating, challenging perfectionism from an early age, and trying to create a family environment in which the "benefits" of having a healthy approach to food far outweigh the "benefits" of having an eating disorder.

Be a good role model

For most of their childhood, parents are the key role models for their children. And even when children seem to be rejecting everything that their parents say and do, in the end it is most likely that they will say and do most of what they have learned from their parents. So the main way to prevent your child from developing an eating disorder is to be a good role model. If you worry about your weight, don't like the way you look, or have a problem with food, then it is highly likely that your child will pick up on this and start to do the same. So try to put your own concerns to one side once you are a parent and be a healthy role model for both body confidence and eating behavior.

Body dissatisfaction   Don't be seen or heard to worry about your body weight or shape. Don't comment on how you look and don't be critical of your child's appearance whether it be weight, hair, or clothes. Picking your battles is key to parenting and how children look is not a battle worth having. Also try to encourage them to see all other aspects of life as more important than just appearance by having hobbies, enjoying friends and family and work. Let them see that how you look is not as important as all the other things you have in your life.

Eating behavior   Eat regularly and healthily, eat as a family, eat in front of and with your children, and be seen to enjoy food in a content and relatively neutral way. If they refuse your food or want to skip meals encourage them to eat but don't make a fuss and be seen to eat your own food without any problems.

Say the right things

Children grow up with a script inside their heads made up of the things they have been told as children. Therefore as adults we might think of ourselves as "lazy," "stupid," "helpful," or "clever" and the chances are this is because our parents called us this as children. I certainly know that I am "particularly good at spotting road signs" and can remember my dad telling me this on many long journeys up north! So give your children positive scripts in their heads relating to body dissatisfaction and eating behavior to prepare them for adulthood.

Give your child a positive script about who they are (© Adam Merrin)

Body dissatisfaction   Help them to grow up in a world where they can be critical of the media and the images they see by saying "look that picture has been airbrushed" or "wow! She's far too thin and looks dreadful." And when someone you know loses too much weight, say "they look ill," and when someone else is a healthy weight, say "they look great!" And for your child, by all means tell them they are beautiful, pretty, or handsome, but try to make more comments on other aspects of who they are by saying "you are so clever," "that story is so creative," "you are a really kind little girl," and "you are just so good with your friends." That way they will realize that looks aren't everything. Then they can grow up knowing that there is much more about them to be proud of and will have a positive script in their heads that isn't dominated by their appearance.

Eating behavior Also try to say the right things about food. Rather than saying "you have been a good girl would you like some chocolate," say "I'm feeling a bit hungry, shall we have a fruit bowl," "I really need some fresh air, let's go out for a walk and have a chat," or "I really feel like some soup for lunch." Food can become the perfect battleground for any child from toddlerhood up to adolescence. If you use food to manage their behavior by giving them sweets when they have been "good" and punishing them by making them miss their pudding, you are teaching them that food is a great source of power and manipulation, and one day they may well turn that back on you. Just offer healthy food and keep your cool when they refuse it. Ignoring unwanted behavior is pretty much always the best way to make it go away, and giving it loads of attention, even if it is bad attention through being cross or upset, will make it more likely to happen again. So keep calm, walk away if necessary, talk to someone else at the table, or just get on with doing something else, and they may well have eaten it when you next look over.

Manage their environment

Although there are many possible causes of eating disorders that can feel uncontrollable, such as genetics, the effects of friends, or the media, some of the main influences come from the home environment and can be managed by parents. Here are some examples.

"When good is better than perfect" This is a great saying that we have on the walls at the university where I work as perfectionism is the main source of problems for our students. Many people with eating disorders are perfectionists and this has often been encouraged by their teachers and parents. Perfectionism may lead to high marks, neat homework, a tidy bedroom, and beautiful drawings, but it can also result in a fear of failure, high levels of anxiety, and eventual paralysis when the child can no longer do anything. If your child shows perfectionist tendencies then do your utmost to counter these from as early an age as possible. So when they get top marks its fine to say "that's wonderful" but when they "only" get 18 out of 20 also say "that's wonderful" and add "everyone makes mistakes

sometimes." When their homework is all beautifully neat, say "that's great" but then sometimes add "Oh! You haven't got time for that now. It's time for tea. It's fine as it is." And sometimes let them hand their homework in late or even not at all so that they learn that the world doesn't explode and we don't all die. Then hopefully they will develop a healthy "good enough" principle which is probably the greatest gift any parent can give to their child.

Managing conflict   Children thrive in calm and happy environments. Ideally we would therefore all have children with people we never found irritating, have plenty of money so we never had to worry about the bills, have a job we loved all the time, and have plenty of support to help us manage to perfect the work–life–parenting balance. Dream on! Life isn't like that for anyone I know, so we all get cross, tired, frustrated, bored, and sometimes even angry and totally exasperated with our lot. But the best way to manage all of this is to keep it away from the children as much as possible. If you need to argue, go for a walk and do it in the park. If you need to let off steam, do it with your friends when you are out and about, and if you are losing it with the kids, take yourself out of the room and go and sit on the loo or have a bath. I used to put myself "on the naughty step" when I knew I was about to say things that I would regret. Then come back in with a new face on and when the kids have gone to bed crash on the sofa and watch a good film.

Pick your fights   Families can't always be conflict-free and shouldn't be. Children need to know that they have crossed a line and boundaries need to be in place so that they have something to kick against. They also need to know when one or other parent has behaved "badly" so that they can learn how to behave appropriately and that "inappropriate behavior" has consequences. Therefore have cross words, arguments, disagreements, or even rows, but pick your fights carefully. A child who is shouted at for not making their bed or leaving the bathroom light on will be immune to the shouts by the time they hit their sister with a stick or tie a rope around her neck. And the teenager who is grounded for a week for having her hair dyed will be immune to any form of discipline when she starts taking drugs or stops coming home at night. Decide "is this a fight I want to have?" and "can I really follow it through?" and if you aren't sure, make your point then walk away. One day you may want the shouting to count for something, but make sure you save it for a day when it really matters.

Living through your children   Two new terms in the parenting literature are "close parenting" and "helicopter parenting" to describe parents who are overly involved in managing and living their children's lives. This seems to be particularly the case when well-educated career women give up their careers to have children and throw themselves into parenting with the same level of conscientiousness that they dedicated to their job. It is also common when parents have a problematic relationship with each other and turn to their children as a substitute. This can place an enormous amount of pressure on children, who feel constantly watched and controlled and may turn to food as a means to regain control. Being a committed parent is a good thing, but it is also a good thing to maintain your life outside of parenting so that you can fulfill your own dreams yourself, rather than wanting your child to fulfill them for you.

Being a parent not a friend   Some children with eating disorders seem to come from families with blurred boundaries where parents behave more as friends than as parents. Parenting is really hard work a lot of the time as you have to behave as you should do, not as you want to do. So you might feel like shouting and lying on the floor kicking your legs in the air (well I do!) but instead you have to calmly say "now please get dressed for school as we need to leave in three minutes." So sometimes it is easier to duck out of parenting and become their friend. This way you can laugh when they are rude rather than be cross, agree with them that school is rubbish, teachers are rubbish, and homework is pointless, and let them stay up late as they are fun to have around. But children have friends to do that with, and so we have to continue being their parents whether we like it or not. And in being parents we set boundaries for our children which make them feel safe and secure, and although they may say they hate the rules and regulations, deep, deep down the structure parents provide gives their life a rhythm and a routine which makes it all feel more controllable and less frightening.

Influence their peer group   Eating disorders are "contagious" and sometimes seem to be more common within certain schools or certain groups of friends. In particular, the numbers of cases of AN seem to be very high in girls' schools and even higher in girls' boarding schools. I am not recommending choosing your child's friends for them *but* if they are starting to show signs of high levels of anxiety and perfectionism, and are beginning to worry about their weight and food, it may be a good idea to try to find them a peer group which is less concerned about these issues. This may mean changing schools. Or it could simply mean encouraging them to join clubs which consist of boys and girls and where body weight is not a factor. Ballet, swimming, dance, rowing, or gymnastics might be ones to avoid. But music, singing, orienteering, drama, scouts/guides, painting, or photography may offer an environment where they have their clothes on and the emphasis is on doing, rather than being looked at.

There are many possible causes of eating disorders. Prevention is therefore difficult and is mostly about being a good role model, saying the right things, and providing your child with a healthy, happy, and structured environment.

How Can Eating Disorders Be Treated?

There are many approaches to treatment and most people with eating disorders will receive some or all of these at some time. They may spend some time in hospital as an inpatient and then continue their treatment as an outpatient while still living at home. They may also join self-help groups run by other people with eating disorders, or see a counselor, psychologist, or their own GP. This chapter will describe three key approaches to treatment: as an inpatient in a hospital; cognitive behavioral therapy (CBT); and family therapy. It will also describe how some of the strategies used by these more formal approaches can be used at home by parents. But the key to treatment success seems to be early detection and getting treatment as soon as possible.

Inpatient treatment

The main reason for treating eating-disordered patients as inpatients is to restore weight. The large majority of inpatients, therefore, are anorexic rather than bulimic, although many also show bulimic symptoms. Treasure, Todd, and Szmukler (61) described the grounds for admission to hospital as follows:

- BMI below 13.5 or a rapid decrease in weight of more than 20 percent in six months
- Lowered blood sugars

- Heart irregularities
- Muscle weakness
- Impaired blood clotting
- Risk of suicide
- Intolerable family situation
- Social isolation
- Failure of outpatient treatment

Fewer patients are currently admitted to hospital than 10 years ago, but inpatient treatment is still regarded as necessary if weight has become dangerously low. Most patients are admitted into age-matched units and nowadays there are units provided for children, adolescents, and adults. Central to the inpatient treatment of anorexia is nursing care which focuses on two factors: the development of a therapeutic alliance between nurse and patient, and weight restoration.

The therapeutic alliance   Patients with anorexia have an overwhelming desire to lose weight and to avoid eating even though their bodies are telling them to eat. Given that the main goal of inpatient treatment is weight gain, developing a therapeutic relationship between patient and nurse can be difficult and requires trust, a belief that the nurse is on the patient's side, and a sense that the relationship is about collaboration. This is developed by the nurse asking respectful questions of the patient, keeping the patient informed about the aims and structure of the ward, and by the nurse interpreting any deceit and aggression as part of the illness, not as a personal assault. The nurse also needs to be firm and consistent in the insistence that the patient's behavior must change. Once a trusting relationship has been developed, this alliance can be used as the forum for interventions such as CBT, which is described later. In particular, within the context of cognitive restructuring (see later) the nurse may address the meanings associated with food avoidance, being thin, and the implications of weight gain.

Weight restoration   Starvation brings with it a preoccupation with food and faulty thinking and is also life-threatening. Weight restoration is therefore essential to the health of the patient and to their ability to engage in other forms of therapy. Inpatient weight restoration involves encouraging the patient to eat regularly, to eat small meals and snacks, and to limit exercise. Food intake usually starts at about 1,000 kcals a day, which is gradually increased to 3,000 kcals, and a target weight range is set according to the patient's weight before the onset of their eating disorder, taking into account the age of onset. A weight increase of 1–2 kg per week is usually the aim, which results in an average admission period of between 12 and 14 weeks.

The process of weight restoration is achieved by using many of the strategies involved in the behavioral components of CBT. For example, meals are taken at a table with other patients and with the nurses. This provides the patient with support from their peers and enables the nurses to provide reinforcement in the form of verbal encouragement and praise. It also provides a forum for the patient to re-learn the pleasures of social eating and to model the normal eating behavior of the nurses. Communal eating also enables patients who are further down the recovery path to support the newer patients, which can promote self-esteem in the healthier patients and provide additional peer reinforcement for the less well individuals. It also enables the nurses to observe and comment upon abnormal eating behaviors such as rumination, cutting up food into tiny pieces, and counting food, and provides a place for these problems to be discussed.

Patients are also weighed regularly. Some clinics tell the patient their weight, with the aim of building trust and active collaboration. Other clinics keep the patient's weight from the patient to minimize a preoccupation with weight and reduce any anxiety caused by weight gain.

The structure of the eating regimen also helps to restructure the patient's faulty thinking. On admission to the ward the nurses will take complete responsibility for the patient's choice of food and the amount eaten. Negotiations about food will be kept to a minimum and nurses will take control of a patient's eating behavior. Many patients are determined not to eat but are being told to eat by their bodies. Handing over responsibility for eating to the nurses enables the patient to eat without feeling the panic of losing control. They can therefore continue in their belief that they are solving their problems and keeping control of their life by not eating, while at the same time consuming food. Gradually, control over eating is handed back to the patient once the patient begins to see that eating, and any accompanying weight gain, does not bring with it the anticipated catastrophic consequences.

Using these techniques at home   Inpatient treatment therefore focuses on a therapeutic alliance between the patient and nurse, and weight gain. It draws upon many of the techniques of CBT and takes away the patient's control over their eating and hands it over to the structure of the ward. Some of these techniques can also be used at home. For example, parents often give their children a choice over what and how much to eat. This may be designed to be respectful of the child's rights but can be experienced as overwhelming and frightening. Therefore, in the same way that the structure of the ward can take responsibility in a hospital, parents can take responsibility at home. From this perspective meal times should be structured and routinized and children who show signs of an eating disorder should be given less, rather than more choice over what they eat. Similarly, communal eating at a family table can provide the time to reinforce healthy eating, and any opportunity for peer support by having a friend for tea can also be a useful source of encouragement and a way to normalize eating. Furthermore, basic reinforcement in the form of sticker charts, money, tickets for pop concerts or clothes, or having friends to stay can all be useful ways to get a child to eat when they are showing problems. We basically live according to a complicated cost/benefit analysis and if parents can make the benefits of healthy eating outweigh the benefits of having an eating disorder, whether it be through praise, encouragement, or outright bribery, then they may be on the way to getting their child back on the right track.

Cognitive behavioral therapy (CBT)

A cognitive behavioral approach to eating disorders involves two core themes. The first is the formation of faulty thoughts about body weight and self-esteem (the cognitive component) and the second is the process of learning via reinforcement, which is reflected in the patient's behavior. Cognitive behavioral therapy is used extensively with bulimia nervosa and addresses both thoughts and behavior. It has been used less widely with anorexia nervosa. CBT for eating disorders usually occurs in the form of a number of stages which apply to both group and individual therapy. These are as follows.

Stage 1: Assessment   The assessment stage involves taking a full history, making any physical investigations, and excluding patients who have a marked suicidal intent or severe physical illness. Extreme emaciation will also prevent a patient from having CBT, which may be offered once weight gain has started.

Stage 2: Introducing the cognitive and behavioral approaches   This stage addresses both the cognitive and behavioral components of eating disorders. For the cognitive component the therapist will describe factors such as:

- The link between thoughts and feelings
- Therapy as a collaboration between patient and therapist
- The patient as scientist and the role of experimentation
- The importance of self-monitoring
- The idea that treatment is about learning a set of skills
- The idea that the therapist is not the expert who will teach the patient how to get better
- The importance of regular feedback by both patient and therapist

The cognitive component emphasizes how beliefs drive behavior.

For the behavioral component the therapist will describe four key factors:

- **Breaking the cycle:** A discussion will be held concerning the cycle of dieting and bingeing, the psychological triggers to bingeing, the importance of eating regularly and frequently, and the cycle of purging and bingeing.
- **Principles of normal eating:** This involves a discussion of the nature of healthy eating, the importance of regular meals, the role of eating in company, planning meals, reducing weighing, and using distraction to take the focus away from food.
- **Diary keeping:** Diary keeping and self-monitoring are central to the CBT approach. The diary can be used to record food eaten and the time and place of any binges, and to monitor mood and feelings of control.
- **Homework:** Patients will be encouraged to do homework and to change their behavior bit by bit. This could involve eating with other people, eating more at each meal, having snacks, or reducing the number of times they purge. This is a form of experimentation and helps to teach the patient that eating can be enjoyable, or at least less threatening, which in turn helps to change the ways in which they think about food. Therefore, by performing the new behavior with no negative consequences, the new behavior will be reinforced, making it more likely to happen again in the future.

The behavioral component emphasizes how behavior drives beliefs and also future behavior.

Stage 3: Cognitive restructuring techniques Central to CBT is the role of faulty thinking such as "if I gain weight I am useless" and "if I cannot stick to my diet I am a complete failure." Cognitive restructuring addresses these cognitions and involves:

- Explaining that faulty thoughts are automatic, believed to be true by the patient, and can influence mood and behavior
- Helping the patient to catch and record their thoughts in a diary
- Challenging these thoughts and replacing them with more helpful ones. This involves the therapist asking "Socratic questions" such as "What evidence do you have to support your thoughts?" and "How would someone else view this situation?" The therapist can use role play and role reversal.
- Introducing the notion of deeper layers of thinking around themes such as control, perfectionism, and guilt, which may be unconscious
- Challenging faulty thinking using role play

Using these techniques at home CBT can be used for inpatients, by counselors or psychologists, in a clinic, or at the patient's home. It focuses on challenging faulty thinking, and encourages healthy behavior through diary keeping and homework. It can also be used by parents to help their children manage their lives. For example, if a child says "No one likes me. I have no friends" they are showing a form of faulty thinking. Using CBT you would say "OK so tell me who doesn't like you?" then list a few names of people who you know do like your child. That way you are providing evidence to contradict the way they see the world. Similarly if they say "everybody says I'm fat," ask them to name the people who have said this, then ask "Did Sarah say you were fat? Did Sophie?" – knowing that these people wouldn't have done so. And again you are challenging their thoughts. Further, if they say "I'm fat and ugly," ask them to look in the mirror with you and ask them how other people would see them. Make sure you choose people who are heavier than them and try to get them to see how they look from someone else's perspective.

Parents can also use the behavioral side of CBT. For example, much as thoughts influence how we behave, the reverse is also true: how we behave influences our thoughts. So make sure you reinforce healthy behavior with praise and attention, and ignore unhealthy behavior if you can. Then when they do show a behavior that is healthy, such as eating with the family or having a good day, make sure this is noticed, commented on, and rewarded through fun and pleasure and anything positive you can throw at it. Then they will start to see the positive consequences of healthy behavior and gradually, bit by bit the unhealthy behavior will reduce and healthier behavior will start to take over.

Seize the moment to do some "sideways talking"

Family therapy

Family therapy emphasizes the meaning of symptoms for the patient and explores the dynamics within the family. It does this using both individual and family sessions depending upon the age of the patient. It is mainly used for patients with AN rather than BN.

The symptoms   During the early stages of family therapy the therapist will emphasize the dangers of food restriction and weight loss, and insist that problems such as continued starvation, bingeing, and vomiting are self-perpetuating, and must stop. For younger patients much family therapy also involves asking the parents to oppose the abnormal eating patterns, to take control of the patient's calorie intake and bulimic symptoms, and to develop a feeding routine that makes the child eat more than their disorder dictates. This approach can at times make the parents feel that they are being blamed for their child's problem but it involves an insistence that something must change and that the parents must make this happen.

Family dynamics   Family therapy also addresses family dynamics. At times, relationships within the families of children with an eating disorder can be enmeshed and overly involved. In addition, the symptoms of the eating disorder can come to dominate the family, creating a focus for the family and a "common concern" which holds the family together. Therefore if the person with an eating disorder starts to recover, the family may feel threatened as they have to learn new ways of interacting. The family therapist can address these issues by announcing any change in the role played by the symptoms and encouraging the family to fill any opening space with new activities and new ways of relating to each other. The therapist can also help to change the family dynamics by challenging and blocking any unhelpful interactions which occur within the family during therapy, supporting particular family members, and pointing out new ways of interacting. The therapist will also encourage clear roles and boundaries within the family and help to establish an alliance between the parents for the sake of effective parenting. For older patients, the therapist will encourage a change in these relationships and suggest that the patient becomes more independent by finding new interests outside the family.

Using these techniques at home   Family therapy focuses on the ways in which members of a family interact to cause and perpetuate a child's eating problems. The best line I remember from a parenting book was "if you want someone else to change, then you have to change yourself." This was a shock at the time, but basically it was saying that a family is a dynamic system. It was also saying that something we are doing is making other people behave as they are, and that since we can't control them, we should start by controlling ourselves. Therefore we might not be able to perform family therapy on our own children but we can explore the dynamics in our families and ask questions such as "how is my child's problem helping the family?" "how are we benefiting from my child's behavior?" "what am I doing to make my child's behavior worse?" "are my partner and I making my child behave the way they do?" and "what is my child achieving by behaving the way they do?" These are difficult questions as they can make parents feel guilty and to blame for their child's behavior. They can also make parents feel angry with each other if they see their partner's behavior as "part of the problem." But in the end we are the parents and so we have to take control. So by changing the way we behave towards our children and towards each other, eventually we can shift the dynamics of the family and maybe the child with an eating problem won't need to have that problem any longer.

Take home points

- There are several approaches to preventing a child from developing an eating disorder.
- These involve being a good role model for healthy eating and body confidence.
- Praise your child for being clever, funny, kind, good at making friends, good at sport, helpful, and funny. *Not* just for being pretty or handsome.
- Encourage a "good-enough principle" and challenge perfectionism.
- Do not live through your children, and be a parent not a friend.
- Eating disorders can be treated in an inpatient clinic or by nurses, counselors, psychiatrists, or psychologists. This encourages weight regain.
- CBT challenges faulty thinking and reinforces healthy behavior using diaries and homework.
- Family therapy explores family dynamics and asks "how is the eating disorder being perpetuated by the family?"
- Many of these "professional" approaches can also be used at home by parents.

In Summary

Eating disorders such as AN and BN are quite rare but have serious health consequences and can be very worrying for patients and their families. There are many factors that may contribute to the development of an eating disorder, which were described in the previous chapter, such as perfectionism, family dynamics, reinforcement, body dissatisfaction, and dieting, but central to many of these is the issue of control, with people turning to food as a means to control their lives. Given these many possible causes, prevention is difficult, but I have outlined some possible approaches. These include being a good role model who gives low priority to body size and shape and models a straightforward relationship with food; saying the right things to give your child a positive script in their heads; and managing their environment in terms of conflicts at home, being a parent not a friend, tackling their perfectionism, and helping them to find a healthy peer group.

This chapter has also described different treatment approaches which are available once an eating disorder has been diagnosed. The most common are: inpatient treatment for those who are severely underweight, with its focus on a therapeutic alliance between the nurse and patient, and weight restoration; CBT, which focuses on beliefs about weight and food, and eating behavior; and family therapy, which highlights the role of the meaning of symptoms and family dynamics. Although such treatments involve highly trained health professionals I have also described how some of these techniques can be used at home, such as taking control over what your child eats, reinforcing healthy eating through praise (or bribery!), being a good role model by having a healthy attitude to your own eating behavior and body size, questioning what is going on in the family that makes your child "need" to have an eating disorder, and asking what their symptoms are really saying about what they need.

Further tips for dealing with issues such as undereating and body dissatisfaction are covered in the second half of this book (see Chapter 13 for managing a child who is undereating and Chapter 14 for a child who thinks they are fat).

Tips and reality

9

"I don't have time to cook"

On my shelf at home are several cookery books designed for mums with endless recipes for pasta dishes, pizzas, casseroles, or sandwiches presented as hedgehogs, cats, clowns, and smiley faces. They are all unused with no evidence of splashed food anywhere! Mums are busy people. Many work as well as having children, and those who stay at home are busy managing the home and seeing to the children. Time is precious. I am not a chef, nor am I a nutritionist or dietician. But I am a psychologist who is bringing up two children and trying my best to put my own theories into practice. Here are some of my own rules of thumb for making your child's diet as healthy as possible and keeping your own sanity.

Cook Whenever You Can

Home-cooked food is pretty much always healthier than eating out or eating takeaways, so try to cook as often as you can. Processed foods, pre-prepared foods, takeaways, and TV dinners may be labeled "low fat," "healthy eating," "low calorie," or "low sugar" but the chances are they are higher in all these ingredients than the food you can cook at home. I don't like cooking, never watch cookery programs, and find cooking a chore. But fortunately children seem happier with simple, easy-to-prepare, quick-to-prepare, and non-fussy meals than with any elaborate meals described by the latest "family friendly" chef. So if you are busy, or don't want to or don't have the time to prepare several courses, then *still* cook but cook simple

The Good Parenting Food Guide: Managing What Children Eat without Making Food a Problem, First Edition. Jane Ogden.
© 2014 John Wiley & Sons, Ltd. Published 2014 by John Wiley & Sons, Ltd.

What do we know: diet and health

- Home-cooked food is nearly always better than ready meals or takeaways.
- Simple meals can take very little time and effort (such as pasta pesto or sausage and mash and peas).
- It takes as much time to boil pasta as to reheat a TV dinner or order in a pizza.
- Eating as a family at the table protects against obesity and encourages healthy eating.

meals that don't take time but are still healthier than anything you could eat out or bring in. At the end of this chapter are a number of meals that my friends and I have put together that have kept our families eating healthily and us sane for the past 14 years.

Find Time

I have a rule of thumb that I will spend no more than 30 minutes every weekday getting food prepared from fridge (or freezer) to table. On two days a week I spend only 20 minutes all in, as my kids have clubs to get to. Most ready meals take at least 15 minutes to reheat and takeaways take time to order in, collect, or wait for them to be delivered. I have therefore become very efficient at working out how to cook quick meals which are still healthy. They may not be particularly exciting and certainly wouldn't make it onto any TV show, but they are good enough. So set a time each day for dinner, work out how much time you have to prepare something, remind yourself that home cooking is pretty much always better than what you can buy in, and start chopping.

Buy Ingredients Not Meals

When you shop, buy ingredients rather than meals and that way you will pretty much always have something in the house to cook. Basic ingredients that I think every weekly shop should include are:

For your cupboard: potatoes, brown bread, brown pasta, brown rice, tinned tomatoes, several jars of pesto, baked beans.

For your fridge: cheese, bacon, sausages (meat or veggie), ham, cucumber, red peppers, carrots, onions, tomatoes.

For your freezer: chicken breasts, frozen peas, beans, broccoli and cauliflower, minced lamb or beef, meatballs, fish fingers.

These ingredients will then provide you with many possible meals that can keep you going through the week. And they will keep you going much longer than if you buy ready meals or processed foods.

Buy ingredients not meals

Shop for the Week

Whether you shop online or go out, try to shop for the whole week rather than just a few days. That way you won't run out of food to cook and will be able to keep going for longer. Also, try to share the workload with your partner. If you do the cooking then get them to do the shopping. It can be done at any time throughout the week including weekends and evenings, and if you are not convinced they will buy the right things, give them a detailed list until they get the hang of it. If you are on your own, then it is more difficult, but try shopping online and make sure you still buy plenty of ingredients rather than meals, to make it all last longer.

Make Life Easy for Yourself

Healthy food does not have to be complicated or time consuming to prepare. In fact, it is often the most unhealthy foods which take the most effort. So make life easy for yourself by preparing simple meals. There is nothing wrong with foods such as sausages, mash, and peas, or pasta and pesto sauce, or pasta and bacon and cheese, or chicken and rice and beans. And fish fingers and oven chips, baked beans on toast, jacket potatoes and cheese and beans are all fine. Just make sure that you add vegetables such as chopped cucumber, peppers, carrots, or tomatoes on the side, and your family will have a quick healthy meal and you will have kept your sanity.

Prepare Food in Advance

Freezers are a great invention. When you have time, bulk-cook shepherd's pie, fish pie, or just bolognese sauce. Or when you are cooking the evening meal simply make double the quantity, to have next week. Then, when preparation time is short, get it out of the freezer in the morning and the evening meal can be quickly reheated when you get back. In fact, most cookers now have a timer, so you can set it all up to go when you leave in the morning.

Roll Meals Over from One Day to the Next

As part of my efficiency drive I have discovered the art of rolling one meal over to the next. So if one day we are having sausages and mash I cook twice the amount of mash, and the next day we have shepherd's pie or fish pie as the mash is already made. Or if we are having spaghetti bolognese I cook twice the amount of bolognese sauce, freeze it, and have lasagne or chilli a few days later. I also cook extra boiled potatoes so that the next day we can have them fried, and if we have a roast at the weekend I keep the meat to go with rice on the Monday. If you are weaning a baby, then leftover vegetables are great for them to munch on. Older children might get bored if you serve the same meal on two consecutive days, but if you serve the same food but disguised as another meal they don't notice.

Have "Help Yourself" Meals

Some days I have run out of steam and feel so bored with cooking. Then we have "help yourself" meals. This involves putting bread, butter, cucumber, chopped carrots, tomatoes, ham, peppers, cheese, and hummus and any old leftovers from the fridge on the table and asking everyone to help themselves. The kids see it as a real picnic treat and it is about as efficient as you can get.

Cut Corners

There are some things that I do that some people would be horrified by, but they make my life easier.

- I never peel potatoes but chop them up as they are, and we are all used to mash with skin in it.
- I rarely peel carrots but just wash them first.
- I never peel mushrooms.
- I microwave meat to defrost it even though it says not to.
- I put pans on the table for serving rather than put food in bowls.
- We eat a lot of frozen vegetables with everything.

Eat as a Family at a Table (If You Can)

Family meals have been shown to be helpful in so many ways. They encourage children who are not keen on eating to eat more and they discourage those who would gorge themselves from overeating. They also enable children to see food as a social event that takes place at a table at set times of the day, which prevents snacking, grazing, and mindless eating. And they offer a time when everyone can take a break from their busy lives and chat about the day. In addition, as a parent you can use the family meal as a time to be a good role model for your child and be seen to try new foods, enjoy healthy foods, and get pleasure from seeing them eating healthily. While you are preparing the dinner, get the children to set the table. This can save you time and get them involved in the cooking process.

Give Yourself Days Off

Seven days a week is a lot to fill with healthy meals and can become a real chore and a source of resentment if you are not careful. So give yourself some days off. Takeaways or ready meals are not great as they are mostly full of salt and preservatives. But every now and then they do no harm. So when you have had enough, reheat a pizza, call in a curry, or have fish and chips. But try to add a salad on the side or cook some frozen peas. And why not get someone else in the household to cook? If your kids are old enough give them a day a week when dinner is their responsibility, or make sure your partner cooks whenever they can. Parenting is a marathon not a sprint and trying to be good all the time just leads to burnout. It's all about finding a way to be a parent that is sustainable and this involves having a strong "good enough" principle rather than aiming for perfection.

Share the Load

Try to get children involved from an early age. Small children can weigh out pasta, mix a salad, or just take their plates through to the kitchen once they have finished. When they are old enough get them to stack the dishwasher or do the washing up. And when they are of age make the rule "whoever cooks doesn't do the washing up." Little bits of help here and there make the whole process more manageable and stop the resentment brewing up. It also sets good habits for adulthood.

Make It Your Space

Some mums like to have their children help with chopping or mixing and for them to be involved with meal times. But I think it is also nice to have some space and be on my own. So get the children occupied next door, put your music on, and revel in the peace! If cooking also becomes a moment of space then it will feel like less of a chore.

What can we do?

- Cook whenever you can.
- Keep it simple.
- Buy ingredients not meals and buy plenty of basics.
- Keep your sanity by sharing the load or having days off and having "easy teas."
- Use tricks such as rolling mashed potato over two days for sausage and mash then fish pie, or bulk-cook bolognese sauce and freeze for chilli, shepherd's pie, or spaghetti bolognese.

Buy ingredients not meals (© Adam Merrin)

Some Recipes for You

I hope it is now clear I am not a chef nor am I a nutritionist or a dietician. Nor do I really like cooking. But over the years I have asked my friends for advice on what to cook that is easy and healthy and that we can all eat together. Here are some simple meals we have come up with that work when time is short and life is busy. I have classified them in terms of preparation time (effort) *and* cooking time (fridge to table) as some meals require you to be in the kitchen the whole time while others involve putting things on to cook, then having time to do something else. You can mix and match the different meals but each meal should have a base of carbohydrate (bread/pasta/potato/rice) and at least two vegetables. If you don't eat meat then you can substitute another source of protein such as soya-based sausages or mince, or pulses. I have described the quantities for a family of two adults and two children who eat almost the same amount as adults. And my top tips:

1.   Get a decent pair of kitchen scissors for cutting meat and fish.
2.   Put the oven and/or kettle on before you start.
3.   Keep grated cheese in the fridge ready to go.

---

1. Sausages, Mash, and Peas (and Onion Gravy)

Time

Fridge to table: 1 hour
Effort: 15 mins

Ingredients

3 sausages per person
2 big potatoes per person
Frozen peas
1 onion (for onion gravy – optional)

Procedure

Put oven on (190°C)
Put kettle on
Place sausages on tray in oven for 50 mins (defrost first in microwave if frozen)
After 40 mins . . .
Chop up potatoes into small cubes
Boil potatoes for 15 mins
Place peas in bowl in microwave and cook for 8 mins
Strain potatoes, add splash of milk, knob of butter, and mash up
Chop onion lengthways and fry with a splash of oil until a bit burnt, add water
Serve . . .

2. Sausages, Potato Wedges, and Vegetables

Time

Fridge to table: 1 hour
Effort: 10 mins

Ingredients

3 sausages per person
3 potatoes per person
Frozen vegetables (peas, beans, broccoli, cauliflower, spinach)

Procedure

Put oven on (190°C)
Place sausages on tray in oven for 50 mins (defrost first in microwave
  if frozen)
Slice potatoes lengthwise into wedges
Place wedges in freezer bag, drizzle in a splash of oil, shake bag a bit
Place wedges on tray in oven, turn after 20 mins
Wait 40 mins . . .
Cook frozen vegetables in microwave for 8 mins
Serve . . .

3. Sausage Casserole

Time

Fridge to table: 1 hour
Effort: 20 mins

Ingredients

3 sausages per person
1 onion
I tin of chopped tomatoes
1 tin of beans
Tabasco/Worcestershire sauce
Frozen vegetables (peas, broccoli, cauliflower)
Can be served with mash or wedges

Procedure

Put oven on (190°C)
Chop onion into small pieces and fry with a splash of oil
Add sausages until browned
Transfer to oven dish with lid
Add tinned tomatoes, tin of beans, and tabasco/Worcestershire sauce
Place in oven for 40 mins
Wait 30 mins
Cook frozen vegetables in microwave for 8 mins
Serve . . .

4. Chicken, Bacon, Mushrooms, and Rice

Time

Fridge to table: 30 mins
Effort: 30 mins

Ingredients

1 large chicken breast per person
1 bacon slice per person
5 mushrooms
60 g brown rice per person
Rosemary and garlic for flavor
Large tablespoon of crème fraîche for sauce
Frozen beans

Procedure

Put kettle on
Put rice in pan and boil for 30 mins
Chop bacon and chicken into bite-size pieces and fry with a splash
    of oil
Add garlic
After 20 mins add sliced mushrooms
Add rosemary
Cook beans in microwave for 8 mins
Add crème fraîche to chicken
Drain rice
Serve . . .

5. Lemon Chicken and Rice

Time

Fridge to table: 30 mins
Effort: 20 mins

Ingredients

1 large chicken breast per person
Dessertspoon of flour
Lemon juice
60 g brown rice per person
Frozen vegetables (peas, beans, broccoli, cauliflower)

Procedure

Put kettle on
Put rice in pan and boil for 30 mins
Slice chicken into bite-size pieces
Put flour on plate
Roll chicken pieces in flour and shallow fry with a splash of oil
Squirt lemon over chicken
Cook until lightly browned (20 mins)
Cook vegetables in microwave
Drain rice
Serve . . .

6. Chicken Kebabs and Cheesy Potatoes

Time

Fridge to table: 20 mins
Effort: 20 mins

Ingredients

1 big potato per person
1 large chicken breast per person
1 red pepper
Grated cheese
Frozen vegetables (peas, beans, broccoli, cauliflower, spinach)
Kebab sticks

Procedure

Place potatoes in microwave for 10 mins (until cooked)
Put grill on
Slice chicken into 4 pieces each
Chop pepper into chunks
Thread chicken and pepper onto sticks
Place under grill (not too high) for 10 mins, turning every now and
   again
Slice potatoes in half, lengthways
Scoop out middle of each, leaving skins intact, and place in bowl
Add grated cheese and mix up
Scoop potato mix back into potato skins, drag fork over top
Place under grill for 5 mins until brown
Cook vegetables in microwave
Serve . . .

7. Salmon and Rice

Time

Fridge to table: 30 mins
Effort: 10 mins

Ingredients

1 salmon fillet per person
Lemon juice
60 g brown rice per person
Frozen vegetables (peas, beans, broccoli, cauliflower)

Procedure

Put oven on (190°C)
Put kettle on
Place rice in pan and boil for 30 mins
Place salmon fillets on oven tray and squirt lemon juice on top
    (defrost first in microwave if frozen)
Place salmon in oven for 25 mins
Cook vegetables in microwave for 8 mins
Serve . . .

8. Chilli and Rice

Time

Fridge to table: 30 mins
Effort: 30 mins

Ingredients

1 small bag of lamb mince
1 onion
1 clove of garlic
1 tin of chopped tomatoes
5 mushrooms
1 tin of kidney beans
Tabasco/Worcestershire sauce/teaspoon of chopped chilli
60 g brown rice per person
Frozen vegetables (beans, peas, broccoli, cauliflower)

Procedure

Put kettle on
Place rice in pan and boil for 30 mins
Chop onion and shallow fry with a splash of oil
Add garlic
Add mince (if frozen that's fine)
Stir until mince is brown
Add chilli, tabasco/Worcestershire sauce, tomatoes, kidney beans,
    sliced mushrooms
Cover with lid and cook on low heat for 20 mins
Cook vegetables in microwave
Drain rice
Serve . . .

9. Salmon Pasta

Time

Fridge to table: 20 mins
Effort: 20 mins

Ingredients

1 large onion
1 salmon fillet per person
Teaspoon of chopped chilli (optional)
Crème fraîche
75 g brown pasta per person
Frozen vegetables (peas, beans, broccoli cauliflower)

Procedure

Put kettle on
Chop onion into small pieces
Shallow fry onion in a splash of oil until soft
Chop salmon into bite-size pieces and add to onions (defrost first in microwave if frozen and cut off skin)
Stir until cooked and mash up a bit with spoon (20 mins)
Add chilli (optional)
Place pasta in pan and boil for 10 mins
Cook vegetables in microwave for 8 mins
Add crème fraîche to salmon
Drain pasta
Mix up pasta and salmon
Serve . . .

10. Pasta Pesto

Time

Fridge to table: 15 mins (10 if you have a quick-boil kettle)
Effort: 10 mins

Ingredients

75 g brown pasta per person
Jar of green pesto sauce
Salad: peppers, cucumber, olives, chopped carrots, lettuce, tomatoes

Procedure

Put kettle on
Boil pasta in pan for 10 mins
Chop salad ingredients and place in bowl
Drain pasta
Stir 5 teaspoons of pesto into pasta
Serve . . .

11. Bacon Pasta

Time

Fridge to table: 15 mins (10 if you have a quick-boil kettle)
Effort: 10 mins

Ingredients

75 g brown pasta per person
2 slices unsmoked bacon per person
Grated cheese
Pine nuts (optional)
Salad: peppers, cucumber, olives, chopped carrots, lettuce, tomatoes

Procedure

Put kettle on
Place pasta in pan and boil for 10 mins
Chop bacon and dry fry for 5 mins
Add pine nuts (optional)
Chop up salad ingredients and place in bowl
Drain pasta
Add pasta to bacon, add grated cheese, place on heat, and stir until
    cheese has melted
Serve . . .

12. Seafood Pasta

Time

Fridge to table: 30 mins
Effort: 10 mins

Ingredients

75 g brown pasta per person
1 bag of frozen seafood mix (squid, mussels, cockles, etc.)
1 onion
1 tin of chopped tomatoes
Tabasco/Worcestershire sauce/teaspoon of chopped chilli (optional)
Salad: peppers, cucumber, olives, chopped carrots, lettuce, tomatoes

Procedure

Put kettle on
Chop onion into small pieces
Fry onion in a splash of oil until soft
Add tinned tomatoes
Add frozen seafood (doesn't need defrosting)
Add tabasco/Worcestershire sauce/chilli (optional)
Stir then cover with lid and leave to simmer for 20 mins
Chop salad ingredients and place in bowl
Place pasta in pan and boil for 10 mins
Drain pasta
Serve . . .

13. Spaghetti Bolognese

Time

Fridge to table: 30 mins
Effort: 30 mins

Ingredients

1 small bag of beef or lamb mince
1 onion
1 clove of garlic
1 tin of chopped tomatoes
5 mushrooms
Tabasco/Worcestershire sauce/teaspoon of chopped chilli (optional)
75 g brown spaghetti (or other pasta) per person
Frozen vegetables (beans, peas, broccoli, cauliflower)

Procedure

Chop onion and shallow fry with a splash of oil
Add garlic
Add mince (if frozen that's fine)
Stir until mince is brown
Add chilli, tabasco/Worcestershire sauce, tomatoes, sliced
    mushrooms
Cover with lid and cook on low heat for 20 mins
Place pasta in pan and boil for 10 mins
Cook vegetables in microwave for 8 mins
Drain pasta
Serve . . .

14. Meatball Pasta

Time

Fridge to table: 15 mins
Effort: 15 mins

Ingredients

Swedish meatballs (already cooked – 8 per person)
1 onion
1 tin of chopped tomatoes
5 mushrooms
Tabasco/Worcestershire sauce/teaspoon of chopped chilli (optional)
75 g brown pasta per person
Grated cheese
Salad: peppers, cucumber, olives, chopped carrots, lettuce, tomatoes

Procedure

Put kettle on
Place meatballs in bowl and heat in microwave for 10 mins
Place pasta in pan and boil for 10 mins
Chop onion and shallow fry with a splash of oil
Add tomatoes
Add tabasco/Worcestershire sauce/chilli (optional)
Chop salad ingredients and place in bowl
Drain pasta
Mix meatballs and tomato sauce
Serve . . . add grated cheese at table

15. Leek and Bacon Pasta

Time

Fridge to table: 20 mins
Effort: 20 mins

Ingredients

1 leek per person
2 slices of bacon per person
5 mushrooms
Pine nuts (optional)
Grated cheese (cheddar or stilton)
75 g brown pasta per person
Salad: peppers, cucumber, olives, chopped carrots, lettuce, tomatoes

Procedure

Put kettle on
Slice leeks and wash in sieve
Slice bacon and shallow fry leeks with sliced bacon and a splash
    of oil
Add pine nuts (optional)
Place pasta in pan and boil for 10 mins
Chop salad ingredients and place in bowl
Drain pasta
Add pasta to leeks, add grated cheese, and stir until cheese has melted
Serve . . .

16. Stuffed Pasta

Time

Fridge to table: 10 mins
Effort: 10 mins

Ingredients

Fresh stuffed pasta (100 g per person)
Salad: peppers, cucumber, olives, chopped carrots, lettuce, tomatoes
Grated cheese

Procedure

Put kettle on
Place pasta in pan and bring to boil (3 mins)
Chop salad ingredients and put in bowl
Drain pasta
Serve . . . add grated cheese at table

17. Shepherd's Pie

Time

Fridge to table: 1 hour
Effort: 30 mins (although less if using mash from the previous day)

Ingredients

1 small bag of lamb mince
1 onion
1 clove of garlic
1 tin of chopped tomatoes
5 mushrooms
Tabasco/Worcestershire sauce/teaspoon of chopped chilli (optional)
2 big potatoes per person for mash
Knob of butter and splash of milk
Grated cheese
Frozen vegetables (beans, peas, broccoli, cauliflower)

Procedure

Put oven on (190°C)
Put kettle on
Chop potatoes into small cubes and boil for 10 mins
Chop onion and shallow fry with a splash of oil
Add garlic
Add mince (if frozen that's fine)
Stir until mince is brown
Add chilli, tabasco/Worcestershire sauce, tomatoes, sliced mushrooms
Cover with lid and cook on low heat for 20 mins
Drain potatoes, add knob of butter and splash of milk, and mash up
Place mince in large deep dish
Spoon mashed potatoes on top
Sprinkle grated cheese on top
Place in oven for 30 mins
Cook vegetables in microwave (8 mins)
Serve . . .

18. Fish Pie

Time

Fridge to table: 1 hour
Effort: 30 mins (feels a bit frantic although less so if using mash from
   the previous day)

Ingredients

Fish mix:
2 pots of fish pie mix
1 onion
White sauce:
100 g butter
4 dessertspoons of brown flour

Half a pint of milk
Mashed potato:
2 big potatoes per person
Knob of butter
Splash of milk
Grated cheese

Procedure

Put the oven on (190°C)
Put kettle on
Chop potatoes into cubes and
   boil for 10 mins
Fish mix:
Chop the onion and shallow fry
   until soft
Add the fish pie mix (if frozen
   that's fine)
Stir until bubbling then add lid
   and cook for 20 mins
White sauce:
Melt 100 g butter in saucepan
Add the flour and stir and cook
   for about a minute
Take off heat and slowly, slowly
   add the milk

Bring back to the boil
Mashed potatoes:
Drain potatoes
Add knob of butter and splash of
   milk
Mash up
Putting it together:
Put fish mix in large deep oven
   dish
Add white sauce on top
Spoon mash on next
Run a fork over the top then
   sprinkle with grated cheese
Cook in oven for 30 mins
Cook vegetables in microwave
   (8 mins)
Serve . . .

19. Meals for When You Have Had Enough

Sometimes it all just seems like too much effort! So here are some quick meals to help you keep your sanity. My motto is to aim high then you have further to fall when you can't manage it any more. So cook these meals every now and again but try to keep them as reserves rather than the mainstay of the family meals. And when you do cook them you can still make them OK by always adding vegetables or salad.

- Fish fingers, chips (or potato wedges), and frozen vegetables
- Jacket potatoes and cheese and beans with frozen vegetables
- Help yourself tea – brown bread, cheese, ham, hummus, salad (peppers, cucumber, olives, chopped carrots, lettuce, tomatoes), leftovers
- Pizza with salad and garlic bread
- Burgers and potato wedges and salad
- Chicken kiev, potato wedges, and frozen vegetables
- Fish and chips and peas

In Summary

We have to eat and we have to feed our children. This can feel like a real chore and often people feel that they just don't have time to cook. I hope this chapter has illustrated how cooking for a family does not need to take up a lot of time or effort, and that if you shop for ingredients rather than meals it is possible to rustle up a meal which is healthy and filling (even if not very exciting) and still keep your sanity.

10

"My child won't eat a healthy diet"

Chapter 1 described how a child's diet should be high in fruit and vegetables, high in complex carbohydrates such as brown bread, brown pasta, and brown rice, and relatively low in fat and sugary foods. It should also be low in salt. Chapter 1 also described how many children's diets are not healthy and are often particularly high in fat and salt and contain far too little fruit and vegetables. So how do you get your child to eat a healthy diet?

Tips for Getting Them to Eat More Healthily

Children often announce food preferences out of the blue and say "I don't like peas," "I don't like potatoes," or "I don't like fruit." Here are some basic strategies for making sure your children eat plenty of fruit and vegetables and a diet high in complex carbohydrates and relatively low in fat. I have also included some tips on how to limit the sugary foods they eat.

Fruit

Eating fruit is good for children, even between meals. It helps them grow, concentrate, and develop a healthy mind and body. Here are some simple ways to get them to eat more.

The Good Parenting Food Guide: Managing What Children Eat without Making Food a Problem, First Edition. Jane Ogden.
© 2014 John Wiley & Sons, Ltd. Published 2014 by John Wiley & Sons, Ltd.

What do we know: the role of diet

- We are what we eat.
- A healthy diet is important for growth and development in childhood.
- What we eat as children impacts upon our health as adults.
- A poor diet is linked to heart disease, diabetes and cancer.
- Being overweight as a child can lead to anxiety, teasing, diabetes, asthma, and feeling tired.

Buy fruit

Buy fruit and bring it into the house! Children like to graze and grab food when they are hungry. If there are bags of crisps around they will grab these. But if there is fruit then this is what they will find when they are hungry. Grapes, satsumas, small bananas, and small apples are particularly popular as they are easy to hold and carry around and are about the right size for small hands.

Get a fruit bowl

So buy grapes, satsumas, small bananas, and apples and place them in a fruit bowl. Then put the fruit bowl in a central place where your children can reach it whenever they feel hungry. Ideally this is somewhere they walk past regularly, and at child level. Snacking between meals is not a great habit to get into but eating fruit between meals is fine and it is a good way to get children to eat fruit when they are feeling hungry. Just make sure they clean their teeth properly as I know dentists have a problem with fruit.

Use mindless eating in a good way

Try giving your child a bowl of chopped-up fruit when they are watching TV. Make it a treat, put it in a nice bowl, and say "here's a lovely fruit bowl for you," and watch it disappear as they make their way through it without thinking. People often show "mindless eating" and eat food without really registering it. This can make people overeat as they eat according to the size of the portion or whether it is there rather than whether or not they are actually hungry. That's why we eat all of the "grab bag" of crisps rather than just the smaller 30 g we used to eat. But for children we can make use of mindless eating, and giving them a bowl of fruit while they are busy watching TV or playing a computer game is an easy way to improve their diet.

Use mindless eating in a good way (© Adam Merrin)

Make fruit your pudding

Try not to have puddings after every meal, but occasionally have a special treat of pudding (say twice a week) and make sure this has fruit in it. This could be fruit crumble, fruit and custard, fruit and yoghurt, fruit cake, or just a chopped-up pineapple or mango. But make it seem special so that fruit is seen as a treat.

Packed lunches

If your child has packed lunches then make sure every day their lunch has some form of fruit in it. Grapes are the easiest in a little pot, but an apple, satsuma, or banana is also good. Even if they don't eat it every day, persist, as they will start to learn that a lunch isn't complete unless it consists of fruit as well as everything else.

Drink it

Nowadays there are a number of ways to drink fruit. Buy fruit juice rather than squash, water it down if it's too strong, and give your children a glass with their breakfast. Dentists suggest only drinking juice with meals to protect teeth, and watered-down juice is less acidic. I personally prefer my children to drink water with their lunch and dinner as I don't think all meals should be made to be sweet. So I would recommend juice for breakfast and water for other meals. There are also now fruit smoothies, fruit cartons, and fruit sachets, which are an easy way to get children to eat fruit. But don't overdo these as they are bad for their teeth. In addition, drinks which are actually food and contain quite a lot of calories are not a good habit to get into as the calorie content of a drink is less likely to be registered than if it's eaten as a food. This can encourage overeating as people forget the "drinks" they have had which are actually "meals." This is OK for small children but as adults we live in a world of high calorie drinks from many different popular fast food outlets and may not realize that the "drink" actually counts as food and is adding to our energy intake. It's always better to eat food than drink it.

Vegetables

Children need a variety of vegetables in their diet. Here are some ways to get them to eat more.

Buy vegetables

You are in charge of the money, the shopping, and the cooking. They are not. So buy vegetables and bring them into the house. Then give them to your children. They cannot eat vegetables if they are not on offer. Always have a supply of frozen peas, beans, and broccoli in the freezer and a cucumber and carrots in the fridge. Children seem to like these the most so always give these at meals. If you are trying a new vegetable, include it as well as one they like so at least they get something, and this takes the pressure off having to eat something different.

Persist

Make sure every meal has vegetables with it. Even if they get left, persist and keep giving them to your child. Eventually they will give in *and* they will learn that a meal isn't complete unless it consists of some sort of vegetable. If they say "I don't like broccoli" still put one piece on their plate. One day they will just eat it. This is particularly effective if they have a friend round for tea. If their friend eats their broccoli your child will too.

Be a good role model

Eat with your children as much as possible and comment on how nice the vegetables are. So don't say "eat your beans, they are good for you." Say "have some beans, they are really juicy." Then be seen to eat your own vegetables and enjoy them.

Raw vegetables

Many children prefer their vegetables raw and crunchy. So give them uncooked carrots or peppers even if you are eating yours cooked.

Make them a treat

Frozen peas in a bowl in front of the TV will get eaten mindlessly. If you say "would you like a lovely bowl of frozen peas" they will feel that they are being treated and eat their vegetables without even noticing.

Hide them

Many mums hide vegetables in their food so children eat them without even knowing they are doing so. Use tomato-based sauces whenever you can, grate carrots into spaghetti bolognese, and add finely chopped onions and peppers in shepherd's pie.

Use peer pressure

When they are going to a friend's for tea never tell the mum "they don't like x," and when the mum asks "what do they like?" always answer "feed them whatever you were going to cook." Children may well not eat cauliflower/broccoli/beans at home but strangely will wolf them down when at a friend's house. Likewise when you have children back for tea give all the children the same food and even use it as a time to cook a food you know your child says they don't like. If their friend eats it, then they may well eat it as well.

Have friends for tea and use peer pressure

Let them choose

If you take your kids shopping then let them choose a new vegetable as a treat. Then cook it. They might be more likely to try it if they have chosen it.

Catch them when they are hungry

Before tea my children become "fridge magnets" and start to hang around looking for food. Take advantage of this and give them a bowl of frozen peas or carrot sticks to munch on.

Drink them

Nowadays there are vegetable juices that children like. Give them these for their packed lunch. But don't be overly reliant on drinking. As with fruit, it is always better to eat food than to drink it, as that way the food gets registered as food and we feel more full afterwards. Drinks can have hidden calories and can prompt overeating if people don't realize that the drink they had in the car was actually half a meal.

Complex Carbohydrates

Children need a diet high in complex carbohydrates to give them energy and help them grow. Complex carbohydrates most commonly come in the form of bread, potatoes, pasta, and rice and should form the main ingredient of any meal. As a general rule *brown* is far better than white because brown bread, brown pasta, and brown rice release their energy more slowly, filling us up for longer and sustaining us between meals. In contrast, their white equivalents give us a quick fix and a sugar high, which quickly declines, leaving us feeling hungry and ready to eat again. So how do you get your child to eat *brown* complex carbohydrates?

Buy them

Children can only eat the food you buy. So buy brown bread, brown pasta, and brown rice and bring them into your house. If your children are very small then just feed them these from the start and they will never know that there is an alternative. Brown should be the norm and they will like them, eat them, and comment when other people eat the horrible white versions.

If you are trying to introduce brown bread/rice/pasta into the house, here are ways to do it effectively.

Don't mention it

At its simplest, if you don't mention that the pasta/rice/bread are now brown then children won't notice the difference. They actually don't taste that different, particularly when covered in sauce or toasted and buttered.

Mix it up

If you feel that your children are more sensitive to such things then mix it up for a while. Cook pasta that is half white and half brown and see how they get on. You could mix brown pasta in with orange and green pasta so it is all just a different color, and the chances are they will eat it. Nowadays there is even wholemeal bread that looks white that you could use. Then after a while tell them "by the way that's brown bread you've been eating" and shift to the proper thing.

Be a good role model

Don't say "we are going to eat brown bread as it's healthier." Health doesn't really work as a motivation for children as it's too long-term and they live in the present. Be positive and say "this bread is much more filling" or "this pasta goes much better with this sauce" or "this rice is much less mooshy than the other rice," or just "ooh this is lovely." Then eat your food with pleasure in front of them.

Make it the norm

Children eat what is given to them and what they are familiar with. Don't offer them a choice, just always buy and cook brown foods, and they will eat them. Cook them when other children come for tea and eat them yourself. And when you eat out, if the pasta or bread is white, don't say "ooh what a treat! White bread at last," say "this is much less tasty than what we have at home."

Choose the version most similar to what they are used to

If they have always eaten sliced white bread it will be more difficult to introduce a dense, seeded wholemeal loaf, so start with a sliced wholemeal loaf that looks and feels more like what they are used to. Similarly, start with a fine brown rice rather than a thick nutty one, and brown pasta which is similar in shape to their normal pasta. This way they probably won't even notice the difference. But if they do complain, persist and make positive noises about how nice it is as you eat it.

Persistence

Keeping going is always the key. Children like what they know and know what they get. And some don't like change. But if you just persist, very soon what they know will shift and so will what they like, particularly if you eat with them and show them that you like the food you want them to eat.

Potatoes

Officially, according to nutritionists potatoes are not complex carbohydrates but simple carbohydrates. They therefore release their energy quickly

What do we know: what children should eat

- Lots of fruit and vegetables
- Lots of brown bread, pasta, rice
- Some meat and fish
- Not many sweet sugary foods or those high in fat
- A diet low in salt
- A varied diet

and don't keep us as full as complex carbohydrates. *But* I think the simple potato has a very important role in our diet as potatoes are full of vitamins and minerals (and have been since they were brought all the way back from South America). So eat potatoes in all their forms throughout the week, but try to mix it up and have boiled, mashed, and jacket potatoes as well as chips.

Give them variety

Each meal should have a complex carbohydrate in it for energy and growth. But mix it up and make sure you use potatoes, rice, pasta, and bread across your meals, to stop your children getting bored and to give them the variety they need.

Low Fat

After the age of 5, children should eat a diet relatively low in fat. This does *not* mean a low-fat diet. It means a diet in which fat makes up a smaller percentage than carbohydrates, fruit, or vegetables. So how can this be achieved?

Naturally low-fat foods

Many, many foods are naturally low in fat. In fact, pretty much all fruit and all vegetables, and brown bread, brown pasta, brown rice, potatoes, fish, pulses (chickpeas and lentils), and of course water have no or a very low amount of fat in them. Therefore eating a low-fat diet simply means eating lots of fruit and vegetables and complex carbohydrates. If you do this then your diet will be low in fat.

Adding fat

But we don't just eat bread, pasta, rice, and potatoes, we add fat and have toast and butter, pasta and cheese, rice and curry, and chips cooked in oil. This is completely fine as long as your child's diet is still mostly fruit, vegetables, and complex carbohydrates. Therefore, have toast with some butter (not loads), have mostly pasta (with some cheese), mostly rice (with some curry), and eat your potatoes boiled, mashed, and in their jackets as well as having chips sometimes.

Protein: meat and fish

Children need protein in their diet and a good source is meat and fish. Most meat can easily be made to be low(ish) in fat by simply cutting the fat off. Then try to cook it without adding much fat back in. Grilled, baked, or shallow fried with a small amount of oil is better than deep fried with lots of oil. Fish is mostly naturally low in fat and stays that way if it's not always wrapped in batter and fried. Reduce the frequency of processed meats such as bacon, sausages, and ham as they contain high levels of salt and other preservatives which may be harmful. Also, only eat smoked foods occasionally as they also may be harmful in large quantities.

Low-fat alternatives

The food industry now produces "low-fat" versions of practically every food including fat! But be suspicious. To make milk low in fat they simply take the fat out. But to make ready meals "low-fat" they may well take fat out, but other things are added in, including sugar, artificial fats, and salt. So I personally buy low-fat milk but avoid other more unnatural "low-fat" foods. If you make your own shepherd's pie, pasta and tomato sauce, or chicken stew, then it will be low in fat if you don't add much fat back in. If you buy the processed "low-fat" versions, they may be low in fat but the chances are they are very high in something else.

Sugary Foods

Children do not need sweets, cakes, biscuits, or chocolate to grow and develop. They are not a necessary part of their diet and if they had never been invented children would be fine. They can produce an instant reduction in hunger, which is useful if your child feels starving, but very quickly that sugar high will drop dramatically and your child will feel hungrier than they did before and want more. *But* they exist, children (mostly) like them, and parents like to give them. So how should they be managed?

Keep them out of the house

You shop and cook and choose what comes into the house. If you keep sugary foods out of the house then children can't pester you for them and you can't be tempted to use them to make your child behave.

Choose sugary foods which are foods

Cakes and biscuits are proper foods with sugar in. They have a place in our diet and add to our nutritional intake. Sweets and chocolates are not "food." They are just sugar. Give your child food that is sweet rather than just sweets. And try to give them sugary foods which also contain fruit or complex carbohydrates, such as oat-based bars or biscuits, fruit crumble, fruit puddings, or fruit yoghurts.

Don't make them too special

If you give your child a biscuit and say "aren't you lucky?" or "you have been a good little boy" then they will see biscuits as special, exciting, and a treat. If you share a large ice-cream pudding and bond over how wonderful it is, they will see having ice-cream as a time to be close to their mum and a way to feel good about themselves. But if puddings are mostly fruit-based, and when they are not they are just another course at the end of a meal, they can be enjoyed but without being given extra special status as more important and nicer than the savory foods they have just eaten.

Don't make them forbidden

But don't ban sugary foods, otherwise your child will simply see them as even more special and even more exciting. Sweets exist in the world and

What can we do?

- Buy healthy food
- Cook healthy food
- Make small changes that might not even be noticed
- Get a fruit bowl and put it out
- Be a good role model
- Say the right things about food
- Try, try, try again with healthy food
- Make chat not food the focus of a meal

your child will eat them. If you ban them, when they grow up and want to rebel then food will start to become the perfect way to react against you and make you cross.

Fit them into your life

Have food-based sugary foods such as cakes and biscuits at home, occasionally. But have sweets and chocolate outside of the home, as part of your routine on an occasional basis. A weekly trip to the sweet shop on the way home from school stops sweets becoming forbidden or too special, but keeps them limited and attached to a specific time and place. Or a chocolate cake after lunch at the weekend in your favorite café lets them have what they want, stops them pestering you for it for the rest of the week, and gives it a place in their diet which is limited.

In Summary

Children need a varied diet, high in fruit and vegetables and brown complex carbohydrates with a moderate amount of meat and fish and a small amount of fat and sugar. The best way to achieve this is to cook as much as you can and buy and cook the food you want your children to eat. Persist with healthy food and if at first your child declares they don't like it, try to make it the norm. And be a good role model by eating healthy food in front of them and saying how nice it is. Also try tricks such as giving them fruit and vegetables to eat when they are busy doing something else, cook puddings that are fruit-based and contain real food, hide vegetables in their food if you have to, and allow them to have some sweets outside of the home so as not to make them forbidden.

11

"My child watches too much TV"
Tips for being more active

Exercise is clearly linked with body weight, and being inactive is central to the development and maintenance of obesity as well as other health problems such as diabetes and heart disease. Exercise also has many psychological benefits and can help with mood, self-esteem, confidence, and friendship problems. This chapter will describe the many benefits of exercise. It will then explore why people do or do not do exercise and highlight ways in which both adults and children can become more active.

Why Exercise?

Exercise has both physical and psychological benefits.

The physical benefits of exercise

Physical activity has been shown to improve health in terms of longevity and a wide number of chronic illnesses, particularly heart disease. The evidence for the physical benefits of exercise is as follows:

- Those who exercise each week using up about 2,000 kcals on walking, stair climbing, and sports, live for 2.5 years longer on average than those who only use up 500 kcals per week on these activities.
- Increased activity protects the cardiovascular system by stimulating the muscles that support the heart.
- Increased exercise may increase the electrical activity of the heart.
- Exercise protects against obesity, diabetes, and hypertension which are risk factors for heart attacks and strokes.

The Good Parenting Food Guide: Managing What Children Eat without Making Food a Problem, First Edition. Jane Ogden.
© 2014 John Wiley & Sons, Ltd. Published 2014 by John Wiley & Sons, Ltd.

What do we know: exercise

- Being active protects against many illnesses, such as heart disease, diabetes, arthritis, asthma, and diabetes.
- People who are more active live longer.
- Exercise strengthens bones and muscles.
- Exercise promotes a feeling of well-being and body confidence and reduces anxiety and depression.
- People are active if it fits into their daily lives, if it's fun, and if they can do it with friends.

- Exercise helps to lay down calcium in the bones to prevent bone thinning. This is particularly important for girls who are more at risk of osteoporosis in later life.
- Exercise strengthens muscles, improving body posture, which reduces back pain.
- Exercise improves immune functioning, making the person more able to fight disease.
- Exercise protects against some cancers, particularly colon cancer and breast cancer.
- Exercise helps with the symptoms of arthritis.
- Exercise makes people feel healthier.
- Exercise is an effective treatment for those with chronic fatigue syndrome (CFS, sometimes known as ME).

The psychological benefits of exercise

Exercise also improves psychological well-being. These effects are described below.

Depression: Those who exercise regularly are less depressed than those who do not. In addition, studies show that exercise actually reduces depression and may be a more effective treatment than medication in many cases.

Mood: Research has also explored the impact of exercise on mood in general in terms of positive and negative mood and feelings of pleasure. The results show that exercise makes people generally feel happier. It can, however, make people feel worse at the start, particularly if the exercise is too strenuous for them. This may be why people give up exercising.

The initial dip in their mood combined with pushing themselves too hard may make exercise seem quite unpleasant.

Managing stress: Exercise can be a good distraction from stress as people think "this situation could be stressful but if I exercise I will not have to think about it." Then, once they have learned that exercise can reduce stress, they feel less stressed next time around as they have identified an effective coping strategy that they can call upon: "I coped well last time I was stressed so I know that I will be able to cope in the future." I once taught a doctor who said that skiing was the most relaxing holiday she had ever had. I asked her why, and she said "I was so scared of dying that I couldn't think about work at all. It was wonderful!"

Body image and self-esteem: People who exercise tend to have a better body image and higher self-esteem than those who do not. There are many possible explanations for this including the impact of exercise on mood (which in turn influences body image), changes in actual body shape and size, and changes in energy levels.

Exercise therefore has many physical and psychological benefits. Current recommendations suggest that adults should do 30 minutes of at least moderate physical activity on at least five days a week and that children should exercise for at least 60 minutes every day. But very few people are as active as they should or could be. So how can you motivate your child (and yourself) to be more active?

People do (or do not do) exercise for many reasons. If we understand these reasons then we can understand how to become more active. Below are the many reasons why people exercise, along with tips for encouraging your child to become more active.

Why Do People Do Exercise? (And How Can You Make Your Child Do More?)

Here are the reasons why people do exercise.

"As part of my life"

The main reason for being active is that it is "just part of my life." Therefore, if children walk to school, play in the garden, climb trees, cycle to their friend's house, or play active games at home (rather than sitting in front of the TV or computer), they will be exercising without knowing it and staying healthy with the minimum amount of effort. Similarly, if adults walk to work or at least use public transport, use stairs rather than lifts, walk up escalators, walk to the shops or out for the evening, and reduce sitting at home or work to the minimum, they too will be doing exercise without having to think about it.

TIPS   AS PART OF YOUR LIFE

- Build exercise into your daily life with the children.
- Walk to school if possible, walk to the shops at the weekend, or walk around to friends' houses.
- Try to have active weekends and holidays.
- Turn the TV off and throw the children into the garden.
- Limit computer time.
- Be a good role model.
- Make positive comments about being active such as "isn't it nice to be outdoors," "we have lovely chats when we walk," "parking takes such a long time."

Throw them out into the garden

To be with friends

The second main reason why people do exercise is that it provides social contact. This is why group sports such as football, basketball, and netball are popular with children. It is also why adults join gyms to attend dance, aerobic, or spinning classes – so that they can exercise while being with other people. Exercise is more likely to happen if it is a social activity which brings with it social benefits.

TIPS   TO BE WITH FRIENDS

- Encourage lunchtime and after-school activities.
- Organize with other mums to get your children to do activities together.
- Have friends for tea and throw them all out in the garden.
- Take them to the park with friends when possible.
- Take another family along for weekend walks – the children will stop moaning and run off happily.

Fun

Most exercise campaigns emphasize health benefits and tell people that keeping active is good for your heart, helps you live longer, and helps you to maintain a healthy weight. None of this means anything to children, who live in the present and find it hard to worry about next week, let alone having a heart attack when they are 65. Even adults don't really think about their health until they have symptoms and find they can't climb stairs, sit on the floor, or run for a bus. And even then, they often just accept this and stop trying. We are very bad at "future thinking" and only really concerned with the here and now.

Therefore, the next main reason why people exercise is having fun. If exercise is fun, the benefits of doing it *now* easily outweigh the costs, and it works by making the here and now more enjoyable. For children, group sports are therefore more fun because they are with friends, but other activities such as trampolining, skipping, dancing, climbing trees, or cycling up and down hills are also more fun than just running round the park. For adults, anything with other people is fun, but also activities which involve music, dancing, even driving a simulated motorbike, or which provide the opportunity to flirt with sweaty people, all make the here and now more enjoyable.

```
TIPS   FUN
```

- Talk about exercise in a fun way. Say "was netball fun at school?" "did you enjoy PE today?" "I used to love skipping when I was your age," *not* "was it cold in PE today?" "I used to hate having to play netball," "those PE teachers are mean making you go outside."
- Think of fun and cheap ways to get them active: buy a skipping rope, a ball, even a yo-yo is better than sitting around.
- Play music and dance around with them.
- Get them to put on dance shows.
- Clear a space and get them to do gymnastics.

Costs and Benefits of Exercise

Given that we live very much in the moment, at the time of choosing to be active the benefits need to outweigh the costs. There are, however, many costs that get in the way, such as "it's time consuming," "it's boring," "I'm busy," "I don't like getting sweaty," "I don't like having to change," "it's embarrassing as I'm not very fit," and "it costs too much to join a gym." Exercise therefore needs to be done in a way that avoids all these costs.

```
TIPS   COSTS AND BENEFITS
```

- If your child finds exercise boring, try to find a game they like that is fun – computer games that involve jumping, dancing, or pretend fighting are a good way to get them moving without realizing it.
- If your child feels they don't have time, work out how much time they spend watching TV or playing on a computer, point this out, and make a deal with them to spend half of this in the garden playing basketball or joining in an after-school activity.
- Make sure you make it easier for them to be active and harder for them to just sit: turn the TV off, limit computer games, and suggest an active alternative.
- Get them to walk to school every day if possible.
- Buy a skipping rope for them, or get them a football for the garden.
- And for adults, if you are too busy or can't afford a gym membership, walk briskly round the block twice a week, and ideally get a friend to go with you.

Social Norms

One key factor that determines whether or not people exercise is whether being active is the norm in their family or social group. Research shows that body weight is "contagious" and that friends tend to have similar body weights. In part, this means that people choose to be friends with those who look similar to themselves. But it also suggests that within these friendship groups a norm of body weight has been established, and over time people within the group change their weight to be more similar to that norm. So it is not only married couples who start to look like each other and get fatter or thinner as a couple as time passes, but also friends.

In a similar vein, being active also runs in families and between friends. So if you change job and make new friends who are all quite active, the chances are you will become more active as well. Similarly, if you meet a group of mums through school and they like sitting around eating cake and drinking tea, then you may well start to gain weight.

For children it is no different. If they have active friends, or go to a school where exercise is valued and seen as important, they will become more active. And central to setting this norm are the parents and the family environment. If parents drive everywhere, then children will grow up believing walking is boring and a waste of time. If weekends are spent in front of the TV and holidays are spent lying on a beach, then children will think that this is how their leisure time should be spent. But if parents act as a role model for how fun, useful, exciting, and *normal* exercise is, then children will grow up seeing it as a central part of their lives.

TIPS SOCIAL NORMS

- Be a good role model: be seen to enjoy being active.
- Encourage friendships with active children.
- Use the car less.
- Have an active day every weekend.
- Talk about how nice it is to be active.
- Make being active normal.

Have active holidays

Confidence

Feeling confident is also key to being active. This can involve being confident at sports such as swimming, basketball, football, or tennis. It can also mean feeling confident that you know where the changing rooms are at the local leisure center, knowing how to pay to get in, knowing where to get the bus from, or knowing the route to walk to school. Children who are not used to doing much will feel that being active is frightening, intimidating, and different, which will be a great barrier to becoming more active. The best way to build confidence is simply to do something a few times, congratulate yourself on having done it, and then do it more. For your children, you may need to bribe them in the first instance but bribery is fine if it works and gets them more active.

> ### TIPS CONFIDENCE
>
> - Walk with them to school at first, then walk some of the way, then let them walk alone (if it's not too far).
> - Let them go to the leisure center with their friends.
> - Point out how others around them or people on the TV are being active.
> - Set up a reward system for every time they do something active. This could be something simple such as stickers on a chart, or pasta pieces in a jar. It could be more complex, such as buying a ticket for something they want to go to then making them earn it week by week, or even paying them monthly with pocket money if they achieve the targets you have set. It's bribery really, but it works and it's worth it if they are healthier in the long run.
> - Give them their pocket money in chunks – some for activities and some for whatever they like.

Habit

We are creatures of habit and the best predictor of how we will behave in the future is how we have behaved in the past. Therefore, once a child has started to walk to school, although they may complain at first, this will quickly become a habit and they will stop thinking about it. Similarly, once they have used the stairs a few times when out and about they will soon realize that this is often quicker and less frustrating than waiting behind someone on the escalator or staring at closed lift doors. You can even make it into a race: you get the lift and see if they can beat you by using the stairs (and always make them win!). Habits are set up early in life and very soon become the norm. Try to do this with exercise so that being active throughout the day feels like the normal way to be. Once established, a habit is very difficult to change.

> ### TIPS HABITS
>
> - Start good habits as early as you can.
> - But if you haven't, start them now.
> - To change a habit, make it fun and a game.
> - Talk about how good it is to be active.

What can we do?

- Build activity into your weekly routine by using stairs, walking to school, using the car less, or encouraging after-school activities.
- Make exercise fun with friends or family.
- Find an activity that suits your child.
- Dancing, pretend fighting, active computer games, skipping, or tree climbing are all better than sitting.
- Turn the TV or computer *off*.
- Be a good role model and be seen to enjoy being active.
- Use exercise to help your child manage their emotions.
- Talk about being active in a positive way.

Planning

Much of our behavior is spontaneous and in response to triggers or cues throughout the day. This can lead to unhealthy behavior and the continuation of unhealthy habits. One way to break this pattern is to make clear and explicit plans and to write these down. These then become a kind of contract with yourself and others, and are surprisingly hard to break. Good examples are to plan to walk to school with the children, or walk to work, or walk into town; or to plan to go for a bike ride at the weekend or to go swimming after school. *But* don't make general plans such as "I will walk more" or "I will be more active." Make them as specific as possible, write them down, and stick them on the fridge.

TIPS   PLANNING

Have a list on the fridge which says:

- "I will walk to school with the kids on Tuesday and Thursday this week."
- "We will go swimming after school this Wednesday."
- "This Saturday we will go for a bike ride round the local park at 10.30."
- "On Saturday morning we will all walk into town at 11.00."

Make this list public, tell everyone what you are planning, and then tick things off when you have done them. This way it is far more likely that you will do what you say you are going to do.

Valuing Health

For most people, being healthy is not a great motivator as the benefits are too far in the future and the immediate benefits of being unhealthy (eating cake *now*, watching TV *now*) will always outweigh something in 5 or 10 or even 50 years' time. But some degree of valuing health is bound to influence how we behave and how active our children are. Therefore, try to generate a general feeling that it is good to be active and that health *is* important. You don't need to become a nag or a bore to do this. Just point out other people who are being active or inactive and be seen and heard to believe that health is important.

TIPS   VALUE HEALTH

- Point out how healthy their friends are who play sport.
- Talk about TV personalities who are active and good role models.
- Be a good role model yourself and be seen and heard to enjoy being busy, mobile, and active.
- Make comments such as "isn't it great to be out of the house," "how lovely to be in the fresh air," "I feel so much better after that walk," "wasn't swimming fun," and "we always talk much better when we are out and about."
- If you have a "teachable moment," then use it. So when a family member, friend, or person on the TV gets ill, talk about how this was because they were unhealthy and didn't look after themselves (if this could be true).

Happiness

There is good evidence that exercise is good for our mood. This may take the form of a "runner's high" for those who are very fit, but for most people it's just a sense of happiness, being alive, and a release of stress when we are outdoors in the fresh air and being active. Make sure your children start to think of exercise as a way to manage their emotions, and give them the clear message that exercise can be an excellent way for them to cope with the stresses of their lives.

Use exercise to manage their emotions (© Adam Merrin)

TIPS EXERCISE AND MOOD

- If they are fed up, take them for a walk around the block or encourage them to play outside for a while.
- Make comments such as "go and let off some steam" or "exercise will make you feel better."
- When they seem better, reinforce this and say "see that worked didn't it? Exercise is a great way to get rid of stress."
- Be a good role model and when you are fed up be seen and heard to go for a run or a walk round the block.

In Summary

Being active protects against many illnesses, such as heart disease, diabetes, hypertension, and obesity and it also strengthens bones and muscles. It also has psychological benefits and improves body confidence and well-being and reduces depression and anxiety. In the main, people do exercise because it's part of their weekly routine, it's fun, and they can do it with other people. So children can be encouraged to be more active by taking this into account. Make exercise a part of their daily lives by using the car less, walking to school, using stairs not lifts, and getting them to join after-school activities. Find an activity that suits your child – dancing at home, active computer games, skipping, pretend sword fighting, or tree climbing are all better than just sitting. Turn the TV or computer off, and be a good role model by being seen to enjoy being active and by planning family days out that involve walking rather than watching a film. Finally, encourage them to use exercise to manage their emotions and throw them out into the garden to kick a ball about when they need to let off steam.

12

"My child eats too much"

We live in a modern world where portion sizes are getting bigger and obesity is on the increase. If you feel that your child eats too much and is becoming overweight then it might be time to do something. This chapter will describe how you can decide whether or not you should be worrying about your child. Then, if you should be, it describes some tips to encourage them to eat less. *But* don't put them on a diet as this might make them think about food even more and store up more serious weight problems later on. The last thing you want is to make food into an issue.

Decide If You Need to Worry

I don't agree with having bathroom scales in a house with children as it can make them overly worried about their weight and weight can become the goal rather than health. But at times it can be good to have some hard data and to know if your child is normal weight or not. So weigh your child when you can, but do it casually without making it into a big deal. So if you are staying at someone else's house who has scales, or when you are in the local chemist or at the train station, get everyone to jump on the scales "for fun" and see what they weigh. Next, a few days later, in response to someone saying something about height – "mum have I grown," "Tom's taller than me now," or even "my shoes don't fit" – stand them against the wall and measure their height. Then use the charts in Chapter 5 to find out

The Good Parenting Food Guide: Managing What Children Eat without Making Food a Problem, First Edition. Jane Ogden.
© 2014 John Wiley & Sons, Ltd. Published 2014 by John Wiley & Sons, Ltd.

What do we know: the impact of overweight and obesity

- Obesity is on the increase in children and adults.
- Some people may have a biological predisposition to be overweight.
- *But* the most important factors are overeating and lack of activity.
- Overweight children are more likely to be teased, bullied, anxious, or depressed and to miss school.
- Obesity is also linked with asthma, heart disease, and cancer.

their BMI, without saying anything to them. If their weight is normal, they are fine and you can ignore how much they eat. If they are underweight read Chapter 13. But if they are overweight to any degree then they may be developing a weight problem.

Also consider the following questions:

- Is your child anxious around food?
- Are they overly concerned with how they look?
- Do they ever sneak food from the cupboards when you are not around?
- Do they refuse to eat at meal times then eat on their own later in a guilty way (i.e. at night, in the garden, in their bedroom)?

If your child is overweight and you have answered yes to any of the above then your child might be developing an eating problem. If that is the case then take them to the doctor, as all the evidence indicates that early diagnosis and treatment is the best way forward. If they are just a bit over-weight, then here are some tips for helping them to eat less without making food into an issue.

Don't Put Them on a Diet

Being a bit overweight as a child is not great. But developing a problem with eating as a child may lead to a lifetime of worry and depression. If

---

What can we do: preventing weight gain

- Manage your child's environment: buy and cook healthy food.
- Be a good role model.
- Say the right things about food.
- Reward healthy eating.
- Don't make food into an issue.
- Help them manage their emotions using non-food methods such as talking, friends, or exercise.

---

you think your child is overeating then try all the tips below to get their eating back on track, but don't put them on a diet. Going on a diet ultimately means having to deny yourself foods that you want to eat. This can make those foods seem even more tempting and, in the end, when people break their diet (which most do), they eat even more than they would have done before. So limit your child's food in subtle ways by being a good role model, changing what food you buy, and cooking and planning meals so that they can learn to live with their hunger. But if you put them on a diet you may well make the situation worse and food will become even more of a treat than it ever was. And as time goes on, you may have set your child up for a future of struggling with one of the central aspects of day-to-day life.

Be More Active

Becoming overweight is a balance between energy in (food) and energy out (activity). If you think your child is becoming overweight the simplest way forward is to get them to be more active. Chapter 11 covers this in depth, but go for walks or family bike rides at weekends rather than watching a film, buy them a ball and a skipping rope, throw them out in the garden or street to play, take them to the local park, encourage them to join clubs at school, and show them that you like being active as well. And say the right things about exercise, such as "go out in the garden and let off some steam," "I'm tired, I think I'll go for a walk," and "that bike ride has made me feel so much better."

Be a Good Role Model for Eating

You are your child's key role model for most of their childhood so be a good role model for eating. Eat healthily, eat meals and don't snack, don't skip meals, and have seconds if you are hungry but not if you just feel like it.

Be a Good Role Model for Body Size

Also be a good role model for body size. We live in a world where people are getting fatter and being overweight has become the norm. If you are overweight don't let your child think that this is normal. And *don't* encourage them to think that being overweight runs in your family and that there's nothing you can do about it. Don't moan to your child about your weight but also don't celebrate it. Similarly, if they are overweight, don't criticize them for it but also don't make it something to be proud of.

Say the Right Things

Being a good role model involves saying the right things to give your child some healthy scripts in their head for the future. So don't say "we are all fat in our family. It's just the way we are," as they will believe being overweight is beyond their control and inevitable. Also don't say "I'm so fat. I hate it. It's so ugly" or even "you are getting fat. You'll have no friends." Such criticisms lead to low self-esteem, self-criticism, and possibly comfort eating, which all make the problem even worse. And don't comment on their eating saying "you eat so much," "gosh you can put it away," "you have such a huge appetite," or "you never seem to be full," as these phrases will stick with them and they will start to see them as true and a core part of who they are. But similarly don't praise them saying "my lovely fat daughter," "you are so fat and cuddly," or "it's so nice having someone chubby to

What can we do: helping them lose weight

- Decide whether or not to worry – are they overweight?
- Don't put them on a diet.
- Manage their environment: buy and cook healthy foods.
- Be a good role model.
- Say the right things about food.
- Eat as a family.
- Eat breakfast.

cuddle up to," as they will believe they need to stay overweight in order to be loved.

Mostly it is best to say nothing. But if you are talking about eating and body size, do it about someone else in a more neutral way. So when you see a celebrity of a healthy size, say "she looks lovely," or when a friend comes round who is normal weight, say "she looks really healthy." And positively praise being active and eating well, saying "let's go for a bike ride this weekend. That will be fun" and "this casserole is really nice."

Change Their Environment

Until the age of about 12 you are completely in charge of what your child eats because you do the shopping, drive the car, have the money, and do the cooking. Even after this age most of what they eat is still up to you. So the best way to encourage them to eat less is to change their environment by only buying healthy foods and bringing them into the house. Don't buy fizzy drinks, crisps, or biscuits if you don't want your children to eat them, and cook healthy meals without puddings. And give them decent portions, but don't overload them with their first serving, so that they have to ask if they want more rather than just eating everything that is in front of them. Then without them realizing it they will snack less and eat well and food won't become an issue.

If they must snack, make it healthy

Portion Control

Strangely enough, a large plate half empty feels less than a small plate full of food. So if you feel your child is overeating and you want to limit how much they eat make sure that you have reasonably sized plates – and all have the same plates. That way you will all be able to eat a decent-sized meal and be able to empty your plate without feeling deprived.

Plan Meals

Children get hungry and will graze on whatever is available. But if there is a set time for meals when they know that they will reliably be fed, living with the hunger and waiting for the next meal become easier. So decide to eat at a set time whenever possible, tell your children when and what you are having for tea, and ask them to wait, saying "it is much nicer to be hungry at tea time. You'll enjoy it more."

Help them learn to feel hungry (© Adam Merrin)

Cook Filling Meals

If your child is hungry they will eat in between meals. They will then eat less at meal times, be hungry shortly afterwards, and eat in between meals. It is a vicious cycle. So cook meals that are substantial and filling. Make sure there is plenty of carbohydrate (brown pasta, rice, or bread) to fill them up, and plenty of vegetables and protein. Don't cook foods that are high in fat as these may fill them up in the short term but this won't last. And avoid sugary foods as these will give them an immediate sugar high and a sense of fullness which will quickly drop right down, making them want more sugar to get the high back again.

Eat Breakfast

Breakfast is such an important meal because it kick-starts the metabolism, gets us out of the hibernation state we have been in overnight, and sets us up for the day. If we miss it, we stay sluggish and can't concentrate until lunchtime. So set out breakfast every morning, sit down with the children, and make breakfast a normal part of the daily routine. And get them to drink something.

Eat as a Family

Eating as a family is the easiest way to set up what is healthy and emphasize the idea that healthy is normal. So eat as a family as often as you can, and then you can be a good role model, say the right things, serve out the right food in the right-sized portions, and help to make eating a normal and stress-free part of the family day.

Seize a Moment to Have a Chat

At some point it would be good to have a chat about being overweight and the dangers associated with overeating. But as with talking about undereating (see Chapter 13), if you lecture your child over dinner or nag them in the car they will switch off, ignore you, and get cross. So be more subtle and underhand and seize the moment in a more casual way. When you see someone on the TV who is overweight, say "that can't be healthy, being that size," or when a celebrity is shown having gained a huge amount of weight, say "did you know that being overweight can shorten your life." But don't focus on the hugely obese featured in all the programs designed to shock, as no one relates to these images and they can make people feel "well I'm OK as I'm not as big as them."

Get a Fruit Bowl

Sometimes children get so hungry they can't last between meals, and the best snack available is fruit. So buy a fruit bowl and fill it with fruit and place it in a central place so they can help themselves whenever they walk by. This way they won't need unhealthy snacks but will still be hungry enough when the meal is ready.

In Summary

If you think your child eats too much and is overweight, first find out their BMI and decide whether or not you really need to worry. If they are overweight and seem to be developing a problem with food then seek help, as this is beyond the scope of this book. However, if they just seem to eat too much then this chapter has offered a number of tips to get them to eat less, but without making food into an issue. Don't put them on a diet but try to make them more active, become a good role model, say the right things about food, change their environment without them realizing it, plan meals so that they know when food is coming, and seize the moment in a casual way to have a chat about the problems of being overweight. But do all this in an indirect, non-confrontational way as the last thing you want to do is to make food into an issue and set them off into a future of eating problems.

13

"My child won't eat enough"

Most children in the Western world are far more likely to end up over-weight than underweight and the most common worry is that a child is eating too much. Some parents, however, do worry that their child is underweight and undereating. This chapter will first describe how you can decide whether or not you need to worry about how much your child is eating. It will then describe some tips for how to manage a child who you feel is not eating enough *but* without making food into an issue for them.

Working Out What Is Normal

The first step is to work out what is a normal weight and a normal healthy food intake, and to decide whether or not you need to worry. Babies' weights are often checked against height/weight charts that come from bottle-fed babies in the 1960s and can make health visitors and parents panic that their baby isn't thriving. Food portions are getting bigger and children are getting fatter, causing a shift in what is considered normal, so a skinny (but healthy) child of the 1960s may well look like they are mal-nourished and underweight today. Teenagers can suddenly shoot up and stretch, making them look like beanpoles that need feeding up. And fatter children, or parents of fatter children, may well comment that your child is skinny and in need of a good meal. But all of this does not mean that your child is underweight. It is just a sign of a changing world and the way in which our notion of a healthy body size has shifted over the past few

The Good Parenting Food Guide: Managing What Children Eat without Making Food a Problem, First Edition. Jane Ogden.
© 2014 John Wiley & Sons, Ltd. Published 2014 by John Wiley & Sons, Ltd.

What do we know about eating disorders: consequences and causes

- Eating disorders are serious mental health problems linked with suicide, heart attacks, and digestive and reproductive problems.
- People with eating disorders restrict their food intake, those with AN show severe weight loss, and those with AN and BN may binge eat and/or use laxatives or excessive exercise to control their weight.
- Their causes are complex.
- They are linked with a history of dieting and body dissatisfaction.
- Other risk factors include perfectionism, faulty thinking, family dynamics, and issues of control.

decades. So in order to make a proper judgment, ask yourself the following questions:

- Is my child's BMI in the normal weight range? (Measure your child's height and weight and calculate their BMI using the charts in Chapter 5, but don't make a big thing of it. Wait until you are at someone's house with some scales and get everyone to jump on for the fun of it. Then a few days later suggest you measure everyone's height.)
- Do they seem unwell and more tired than usual?
- Do they seem anxious around food?
- Are they finding excuses not to eat?
- Are they becoming overly concerned with how they look?
- Are they refusing some foods but still eating lots of their favorite foods if you cook them?

You should worry if your child's BMI is below the normal weight range, if they seem unwell, and anxious around food, if they avoid eating with you, and if they are overly worried about how they look. Then you should take them to your doctor. But if they are just a bit skinny and going through a fussy stage, when they will eat plenty if you cook what they like, but announce that they don't like the rest, then the best way forward is to ignore it and see it as a stage they will grow out of.

In general, here are some tips for getting your child to eat more without making food into an issue.

Be a Good Role Model for Eating

Children of all ages learn what and how much to eat from their parents. Up until the age of about 11 parents are their key role models. After this age, even if it starts to feel that their friends are more important and that we are losing our grip, secretly they still watch what their parents do, and, whether they like it or not, they will probably end up like us. So the most important thing you can do is to be a good role model. Eat healthy foods, don't snack, don't overeat or undereat, and be seen to try new foods and enjoy them.

Be a Good Role Model for Body Satisfaction

Be a good role model for how you feel about how you look. If you have issues with your own body size then being a parent is about putting these to one side and not letting your child know about them. Don't complain about being too fat or too thin to your child, don't discuss going on the latest diet, don't comment on the body weight of their friends or your friends, and don't point to a celebrity in a magazine and say "I would love to look like that!" In fact, teach them how fake images in magazines are. Celebrate other aspects of yourself and your child, making the most of how clever, funny, kind, hardworking, sporty, or creative they are. And make them realize that how they look is only one aspect of who they are.

The media lies (© Adam Merrin)

Eat as a Family

Try to eat at the table with the family as often as you can. Eating with others can make eating seem more normal and less of an issue as the focus is less on the food and more on the conversation. But don't make the meal time a chance to nag your children about homework, delve into their private lives, or argue with your partner. Make meal times as easy as possible and a fairly neutral time when people can get together to eat and chat.

Say the Right Things

What you say is almost as important as what you do. So say the right things about food and body size. Eat healthy food and comment "this is lovely," have a second helping saying "this is really lovely," and stop when you are full, saying "I am full now." Don't call healthy food "boring" or even "so healthy." Don't say "I'm still hungry but I mustn't eat any more in case I get fat" and don't comment "I'm stuffed but I'll just have one more helping." Try to talk about food in a way that reinforces eating when you are hungry and stopping when you are full and doesn't make body size into an issue.

Don't Focus on the Food

If your child is undereating and going through a stage of refusing food, don't make their eating behavior the focus of the family. First, don't ask them "would you like some potatoes" or "we are having spaghetti bolognese. Is that OK?" This can make them feel too much in control and gives them too much choice. Cook food you know they like without asking them. Next place it on their plate, the same as everyone else in the family. Then chat, including them in the conversation but without making them the focus of the meal. You may find that by the end of the meal they have eaten what they were given without even thinking about it. Sometimes ignoring a problem does make it go away whereas focusing on it gives it the attention that the child was seeking.

Eat as a family but make the meal about chat not food

Be Encouraging

You can encourage a child to eat more but don't let this dominate a meal. The odd comment such as "try and eat a few more peas" or "have a bit more of your tea or you'll be hungry later on" is fine. But pressure, blackmail, anger, upset, and any kind of drama will make the child dig in their heels and you will have lost the battle. The key advice for parents is "pick your fights carefully." If you say "you are not leaving the table until you have finished your tea," then you may well have a child still sitting there on their own in the middle of the night. And that's not good for anyone!

Cook What They Like

Ideally children should eat what everyone else eats and be flexible enough to fit in with the family. And ideally parents should offer their children a varied diet so that they get to try new foods and get a proper balance of nutrients. But if your child is going through a fussy stage and starts to declare that they don't like what you cook, then take the pressure off for a while and cook what you know they like. So if they like fish fingers, pizza, or even the dreaded chicken nuggets, cook them (for all the family) for a few days, to take the pressure off and remove the focus from food. Ideally, still try to all eat the same, otherwise they may like the attention of being different, and do it casually without a fuss, explaining "we are running out of food" or "I feel like a quick tea tonight." It is not great to feed your child unhealthy food. But it is far, far worse to make food into an issue. So burst the bubble by giving them what they like, and after a week or so, see if the tension has lifted, and go back to your normal way of eating.

Keep It Varied

When children go through a fussy stage, it is easy to give them what they like, then get stuck and feed them the same foods over and over again. But try to remember that children do announce random likes and dislikes which will disappear as quickly as they arrived. So try not to get stuck in a rut and quickly get back into the habit of offering a varied diet again.

Use Mindless Eating

Mindless eating is usually seen as a problem and many people mindlessly eat food just because it's there. But it can also be used to help children eat more healthy foods. So when your child is watching the TV, give them a bowl of chopped-up fruit or a plate of bread, carrot sticks, and cucumber, and they will eat it without thinking.

Seize the Moment to Have a Chat

If your child is not eating enough, at some point it is good to have a chat about eating disorders and how serious they are. You need to emphasize that anorexia has a very high mortality rate and that bingeing can cause long-term harm. But if you lecture them at the dinner table or in the car they will switch off, ignore you, and get cross. The trick is to be more subtle and manipulative. So wait for a time when the subject can come up in a more natural way. This might be due to something on the TV or in a magazine or something they are covering at school. That way when a character in a sitcom develops an eating disorder you can say "anorexia is scary. Did

---

What can we do about eating disorders: prevention

- Check that your child really is underweight.
- Be a good role model for healthy eating and body confidence.
- Don't focus on how they look but praise them for being clever, funny, kind, good at sport, and a good friend.
- Eat as a family.
- Eat breakfast.
- Make chat not food the focus of the family meal.
- Keep conflict away from the children.
- Be their parent not their friend and don't live your life through them.

---

you know it can cause infertility and is more likely to kill you than any other mental health problem?" If you are browsing through a magazine together, say "look at her, she is so thin. She looks dreadful. She'll kill herself if she's not careful." Or you could even play something by the Carpenters and mention that Karen Carpenter died from anorexia and how tragic this was. This may open up a conversation about your child's eating. But if it doesn't that's fine as the seed has been planted and you can revisit it another time.

Question What Is Happening at School

Sometimes problems with friends, school work, teachers, or bullying can cause children to eat less at home. Ask your child how things are going and watch for signs with their friends or ask the teachers to watch out for any problems. Most schools now have excellent pastoral support systems in place, which I have always found really helpful, so go into your child's school and speak to someone. And make sure your child has plenty of opportunities to talk to you. Sometimes this can be easiest when you are out walking, doing the washing up, or at bedtime when things are calmer and less intense than over dinner. "Sideways talking" can be a lot more useful with children than face-to-face talking.

Question What Is Happening in the Family

The family is a system and when one family member starts to have problems it is often because of something someone else has done. For example, if parents are arguing a lot then a child might stop eating to move the focus onto themselves and help the parents bond together. Or if one child excels at sport the other might start refusing to eat to claim back some of the attention. And often children take on the role of "good child" or "bad child" in a family to balance each other out. So if your child starts to have problems around food, question what has changed in the family. Then see if you can change it back.

Consider How You Can Change

It is far easier to change yourself than it is to change someone else. So if your child has problems, see if changing what you do ultimately helps to change what they do. If you are focusing on what they eat, then focus on some other aspect of them: their school work, their friends, their hobbies. If you have tried ignoring their eating behavior, try encouraging them to eat more with praise, sticker charts, or outright bribery. If you cook what you like, then try cooking what they like, and if you always eat as a family, let them have tea in front of the TV for a few days. And if you are always in for them, go out more, or if you go out a lot, start staying in. Break the rules and shake things up a bit and see whether this makes a difference.

Use Peer Pressure

Children like to be like their friends, so use peer pressure to get their eating back on track. Invite friends round for tea and give them all the same food and the same amount to eat. Or get them to make tea with pizza bases and toppings to choose from, or even let them make whatever they like. Try arranging for your child to go to a friend's for tea and ask the mum to feed your child whatever they are feeding theirs but not to make a fuss about it.

What can we do about eating disorders: treatments

- If your child has a real problem with weight and food, seek professional help.
- Possible treatments are inpatient treatment, CBT, or family therapy.
- Some of the skills of these treatments can be used at home by parents.
- Seeing a counselor or a psychologist can also help.
- If you just want them to eat a bit more, then follow all the tips offered for healthy eating.
- Eat as a family.
- Encourage eating without pressure.
- Don't use meal times as a battleground.
- Consider how you can change what *you* do to change what *they* do.

Use Natural Breaks in the Routine

People seem most able to change their behavior following a life event or life crisis such as a relationship breakdown, change of job, or health problem. Although we can't create life events for our children, times when the normal routine of our lives is challenged, such as family get-togethers, after an illness, holidays, or birthdays, can all be a useful opportunity to break any unhealthy habits your child has developed, whether it be under- or overeating. So take advantage of any such events and use them as a chance to get your child to think less about food, worry less about how they look, or find a new healthier approach to eating – but not by making a fuss about what they eat, just by letting the ongoing events shake things up a bit and seeing what happens.

Seek Help

Eating disorders are very rare in children under the age of 12 but more common in teenagers, particularly teenage girls. Most of the evidence indicates that early diagnosis and early intervention work best. If your child is losing weight, has a BMI below the normal weight range, and is starting to become anxious around food, then seek help. I would avoid making food into an issue if your child is just going through a stage or becoming a bit picky about their food. But if your child is developing a problem, professional help way beyond the scope of this book is the best way forward.

In Summary

In terms of probabilities, it is more likely that your child will end up overeating and overweight than undereating and underweight. So the first stage is to decide whether you really have something to worry about or whether your skinny child just looks skinny due to changing social norms in a world that is getting fatter. But if you are worried and think your child needs to eat more, then this chapter has offered some possible ways to encourage your child to eat more without making food into an issue. These include being a good role model by eating well and not publicly worrying about your own body size, saying the right things about eating and weight, having family meals which are more about chat than food, not making food into the focus of the family, encouraging your child to eat more in casual non-confrontational ways, using mindless eating in positive ways, finding out what is happening at school or in the family, changing your own behavior, using peer pressure, and taking advantage of natural breaks in the family routine to make a change. So *do* find ways to encourage your child to eat more if you feel they genuinely are undereating. But don't make food into an issue as this could store up even bigger problems for the future.

14

"My child thinks they are fat"

Many adults don't like the way they look, and women in particular often feel that they are too fat and unattractive. Men can also be dissatisfied with their bodies and often say that they want to be taller or more muscly. Unfortunately children nowadays also have these feelings and both girls and boys as young as 9 have been shown to worry about being fat. But it is not only being too fat that can make them unhappy. Feeling too short, too tall, too skinny, too spotty, having curly hair, or having straight hair, or just feeling different, in a million possible ways, from the way they would like to look, can be upsetting. This chapter will offer some tips on how to manage a child who is critical of how they look, and suggest some ways to shift their attention away from their body onto other aspects of who they are.

Be a Good Role Model

If you criticize how you look to your children then they will do the same. You are their greatest role model and if you have issues about your own body image then being a parent is about trying to put these to one side and presenting a positive front to your child. This is particularly important when they are entering puberty as any concerns they have will start to burst to the surface as their body changes and grows in ways that can feel scary and confusing. So at best make positive comments about yourself. But if you can't manage this, then just say nothing.

The Good Parenting Food Guide: Managing What Children Eat without Making Food a Problem, First Edition. Jane Ogden.
© 2014 John Wiley & Sons, Ltd. Published 2014 by John Wiley & Sons, Ltd.

What can we do?

- Be positive about your own body and those of your friends and family: be a good role model.
- Comment that your child is clever, fun, kind, a good friend, a good runner, or hardworking. *Not* just that they are pretty or handsome.
- Teach them to be critical of the media: point out airbrushing, lighting, and makeup whenever you can.
- Acknowledge their feelings and listen, then focus on the positives.
- Bin the scales, move the mirrors, and don't criticize their clothes or hair.
- Use their peers as a comparison, not fake people in the media.
- Challenge their beliefs.
- Encourage a "good enough" principle.
- Expand their interests and encourage them to be more active.

Say the Right Things about Your Child

It is fine to call your child "pretty," "beautiful," "handsome," or "good looking" sometimes. But try not to make compliments based upon looks the mainstay of how you speak about them. If your daughter is always "mummy's pretty girl" or your son "daddy's handsome boy" then they will grow up valuing how they look above all other aspects of themselves. And then, when they feel that they are no longer "pretty" or "handsome," not only will they have that to worry about, they may also worry that their mum or dad will no longer find them special. So also comment on what they do and what they are, as well as how they look. Tell them that they are clever, funny, kind, caring, hardworking, good at making friends, and thoughtful and then they will have a whole spectrum of characteristics to build their confidence upon.

Say the Right Things about Others

When watching films or TV, reading a book, or just talking about family and friends, try to keep comments about how people look to a minimum. If all comments about celebrities are that they are "too fat," "too thin," "looking old," or "not as pretty in real life" then your child will learn that looks are key to who we are. But if they hear that this celebrity does a lot of work for charity, or that one is a good actor, then the world can become a more balanced place where how we look is just one of many aspects of who we are. At times this can feel like fighting an impossible battle as we are surrounded by so many fake images of "beautiful" people. But if your child gets healthy messages at home then maybe this can undo some of the damage done by all the other sources of information.

Acknowledge Their Feelings

It is true that some children are fatter than others; that some are shorter than their friends; that many get spots; and that quite a few go through a strange stage in puberty when their jaws grow at different rates from their heads or their legs stretch like strings. If your child does not like the way they look, and you can sort of see their point, then you need to acknowledge their feelings but then try to get them to reframe them in a more positive way. So if your child *is* fat and says "I'm fat" or your child is spotty and says "I'm spotty" it's no good saying "no you are not darling, you are lovely." This may feel as if you are being reassuring, but what you are actually doing is denying their experiences and brushing away their feelings. So acknowledge their feelings and say "yes you have put a bit of weight on at the moment" or "yes you are a bit spotty at the moment." Then say "and I guess that must feel a bit difficult," and that way you are acknowledging what they are going through. Then ask them about it, such as "why do you think that is?" and listen. After a while, try to reframe what they are feeling by doing the following: emphasize that it is a stage they are going through and it will probably pass as they grow up; ask for examples of their friends who are also fat/spotty/short, etc., to make them feel that they are not alone; then ask if they know of anyone who went through this stage and came out the other side, to make them realize that things change. Hopefully, this will make them feel listened to and that the problem is not as great as they thought. This is similar to the principles of CBT which are described in Chapter 8, together with some ideas for using this approach at home.

Focus on the Positives

If they are upset about something to do with their appearance and you have had a conversation trying to acknowledge their feelings, then a day or so later start trying to focus on positive aspects of who they are. Be particularly positive about any work they bring home from school or the way they get on with their friends. Mention the fact that they made their bed, were kind to their pets, or even kind to you. And just try to boost them up in general. Even mention something about their appearance saying "your hair looks lovely today" or "your eyes are so blue."

Bin the Scales

I personally have a thing about bathroom scales and think that they are dangerous, particularly for teenagers. So if you have a child who is starting to worry about how they look (or any child, or in fact no child at all!), get rid of the scales. We don't need to know what number the dial says to know whether we have gained or lost weight – our clothes tell us that, or we can go to our GP and be weighed. But that dial in the bathroom can make people obsessed with their weight and have us watching the minute changes, which could easily be due to time of the month, the size of our dinner, or how much we have drunk rather than any actual weight loss or gain. If you desperately still need to know how much you weigh, then pop round to a friend's house or to the chemist, but for the sake of your child, I think the scales should go.

Bin the scales: they can make teenagers obsess about their weight (© Elena Elisseeva / Shutterstock)

Move the Mirrors

I also worry about full-length mirrors in children's bedrooms. I have no evidence for this, and know of no studies that have looked at the effect of mirrors, but I feel that for children to be alone in their rooms, having all the emotions that they have, with a full-length mirror to stare at and scrutinize every aspect of themselves, cannot be healthy. So have them in communal spaces, but – particularly if your child is starting to worry about how they look – move the mirror out of their room and make it that bit harder for them to criticize their body. *But* don't do this in a dramatic way saying "I've had enough of you staring at yourself. This has got to go!" Find an excuse such as "we are having a clear out," "the walls need painting," or "it's better in the guest room where everyone can use it," then move it without them quite knowing why.

Teenagers can spend many hours in front of the mirror – you may have to remove the mirror for a while!

Don't Comment on What They Wear

There are many fights to have with our children and the key to parenting is to pick your fights carefully. What they wear or the style or color of their hair seems to be a fight not worth having. Fashions change so quickly and children so want to be like their peers that it is hard for anyone from a different generation to judge what they look like or what signals they are giving out to their peers. So if your child looks to you like "a beggar," "a thug," or "a tart," or if your son looks like "a girl" and your daughter like "a boy," this may be your interpretation, but to their peer group they may look perfectly fine. When it comes to fashion we are well past the age when we can read what it all means anymore. So it is probably best to keep quiet and save the fight for something more important. And by not commenting on their clothes or their hair we can teach the message that how we look is only a small part of who we are.

Explain the Tricks of the Media

Every day we are bombarded with fake images of how people look. Aging actresses are made to look young, and young, thin, wrinkle-free actresses are made to look even younger, and thinner, with poreless, spotless, perfect skin. This is done through airbrushing, makeup, lighting, body doubles, and computer-generated imagery (CGI). Children need to be taught this so that they don't make comparisons between themselves and something that is just not real. It's bad enough comparing yourself to your thinner friend but at least you know that during PE their thighs wobble and they get spots. But the images in the media present this flawless world which sets unrealistic goals and makes everyone feel inadequate. So next time you are sitting in a café find a magazine and go through it showing your children how the images have been changed, and emphasize how dangerous this can be.

Use Their Peer Group

The best comparisons to make are always with our peer group. So when I worry that I am getting old, I know I'll feel old if I look at my students, but if I compare myself to my same-aged friends, I know I'm doing fine. So when your child is feeling "short" ask them to tell you the names of two children taller than them. Then, if you know them, list the names of four children, of the same age, who are their height or smaller. Similarly, if they feel spotty, ask them about their friends and see who else has spots. And if they feel fat make sure you give them a mix of people to focus on who are both thinner and fatter. That way you can help to take the negativity out of the problem without denying that it exists.

Challenge Their Beliefs

When children are feeling rotten about themselves, they are prone to make grand generalizations, saying "everyone says I'm fat," "no one likes me," "I have no friends," or "everyone is thinner than me." When they do this, help them to change their beliefs by challenging what they think and finding evidence to contradict it. So say "who says you are fat?" Then after they have listed a few names, say "what about Amy?" (who you know wouldn't say this), "does she call you fat? What about Emily or Becca?" And say "so who do you sit with at lunch? Do they like you?" or "you were invited to Tom's party. He must like you." That way it is hard for them to hang on to their black and white view of the world and they will start to see that it is all not as bad as they thought it was. This is also similar to the principles of CBT described in Chapter 8.

Give Them a "Good Enough" Principle

Children and adults who are prone to perfectionism can turn this inwards and start becoming critical of the way they look. As a result, they no longer just want to be the best at school or the best at sports and find it difficult when they make mistakes, they also want to look "perfect." If your child is a perfectionist, challenge this as early as you can by celebrating when they "only" get 16 out of 20 in a test, when they come third in a race, or when they are picked as a reserve for the team. In addition, don't worry if they wear odd socks, if their clothes don't seem to match, or if their hair gets untidy. And treat yourself in the same way, so that they see you

What do we know: body dissatisfaction

- Many men and women are critical of the way they look.
- Children as young as 9 say they feel fat but also that they feel too short, too tall, spotty, or just not like their friends.
- Children often learn their body dissatisfaction from their parents.
- Children can develop a negative script in their heads that lasts the rest of their lives.
- Perfectionism can make people critical of how they look.
- When we are unhappy we tend to make negative comparisons with those around us and feel worse.
- Body dissatisfaction can lead to dieting and, in a minority, dieting can lead to eating disorders.

without makeup, see others seeing you this way, and hear you being happy with the way you look. Perfectionism can be crippling to both children and adults, and a "good enough" principle is about the best gift you have to offer.

Good is better than perfect (© Adam Merrin)

Seize the Moment to Have a Word about Eating Problems

If your child is becoming overly worried about their body size, then you need to have a chat about eating disorders and how dangerous they are. But don't do this in a confrontational way as you remove their mirror from their bedroom or over dinner. Do it in a subtle "sideways" way when you are out walking, or in a café, or when prompted by something on the TV or in a magazine. So don't say "you must stop worrying about your size. It could be dangerous." But do say "gosh look at her. She's so thin. That's really dangerous. People die from eating disorders you know."

Be More Active

Teenage girls, in particular, can become extremely inactive and easily spend their days lying around in their rooms doing their hair or texting their friends. If they are worried about how they look, this can make them worry more and cause them to become even more focused on their appearance. One of the best solutions is simply to get out more and be more active. Try doing more things as a family that involve getting out of the house and going places, whether it be swimming, bowling, going for a walk, or just wandering around the shops. That way they will get distracted and will be less likely to think about themselves, at least for a while.

Expand Their Interests

Try also to get them to take up new hobbies on their own. New clubs or skills will help to build their confidence and shift their attention away from themselves, but choose wisely as some sports, such as ballet or gymnastics, are very body- and mirror-focused. Also get them to do something useful involving helping others. If they are old enough, get them to volunteer at the local soup kitchen, a home for the elderly, with guides, brownies, or scouts, or at a charity shop. Helping others is a great way to take anyone's attention away from feeling fat.

Do Something about It

Finally, some children feel fat because they *are* fat, and being fat is not healthy. Therefore, the time may well come when you need to help them lose some weight. Tips on how to manage a child who is overeating and gaining weight are covered in Chapter 12.

In Summary

Growing up can be a difficult time, particularly puberty and adolescence, when a child's body changes in ways that can be upsetting and scary. If your child starts to criticize the way they look, whether it be feeling fat, spotty, too short, or too tall, this chapter has offered some tips for moving attention onto other aspects of who they are. In particular, being a good role model and saying the right things about body size can help a child to see that we are more than just how we look. Binning the scales and moving full-length mirrors are simple practical measures that might help, and encouraging children to be more active and to take up new activities and hobbies can expand their horizons. And teach them about the tricks of the media and the ways in which the images we see are fake and unreal. But you also need to acknowledge their feelings and make them feel heard, so don't just offer bland reassurances but listen to them and then try to focus on the positive aspects of who they are.

15

Take home points

This book has covered the facts and theories of eating and its related problems. It has also offered tips for managing a number of common issues for parents who are trying to get their children to have a healthy diet while negotiating the pathway between obesity and eating disorders. Across all the different areas, some common themes keep recurring which seem to me to be central to managing what your child eats, without making food an issue. These are: being a good role model, saying the right things, and managing their environment. I have pulled these together with examples in Figure 15.1.

As parents we are in charge. We may not always feel like it, but we have the money, the car, we do the shopping and the cooking, and although we get pestered, bribed, or even bullied to do it their way, we are still in charge, at least for a while. So if you make your home a healthy home, if you are a good role model for how you eat and how you feel about the way you look, and if you say the right things about being active, eating, body size and shape, then you will have done your best to set your child up for the world outside. And hopefully, although they may rebel at points along the way, as they grow up you will have given them a solid start in life that will stay with them forever.

Final Words

I have spent 25 years researching eating behavior and 14 years trying to use at least some of what I have learnt with my own children. I have said and

The Good Parenting Food Guide: Managing What Children Eat without Making Food a Problem, First Edition. Jane Ogden.

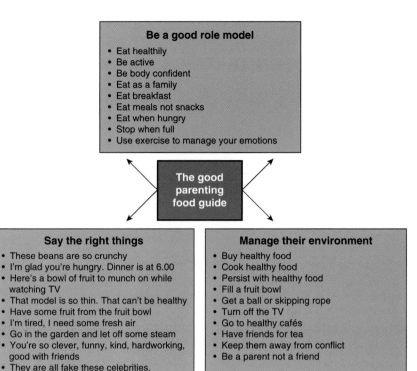

Be a good role model
- Eat healthily
- Be active
- Be body confident
- Eat as a family
- Eat breakfast
- Eat meals not snacks
- Eat when hungry
- Stop when full
- Use exercise to manage your emotions

The good parenting food guide

Say the right things
- These beans are so crunchy
- I'm glad you're hungry. Dinner is at 6.00
- Here's a bowl of fruit to munch on while watching TV
- That model is so thin. That can't be healthy
- Have some fruit from the fruit bowl
- I'm tired, I need some fresh air
- Go in the garden and let off some steam
- You're so clever, funny, kind, hardworking, good with friends
- They are all fake these celebrities. All airbrushed

Manage their environment
- Buy healthy food
- Cook healthy food
- Persist with healthy food
- Fill a fruit bowl
- Get a ball or skipping rope
- Turn off the TV
- Go to healthy cafés
- Have friends for tea
- Keep them away from conflict
- Be a parent not a friend

Figure 15.1 The good parenting guide: summing up

done many things along the way that were not great parenting and I haven't finished yet! But this book is my attempt to put that research into practice and make it available to the real world of parents trying to do a good job. I have also seen many children and adults who have a real problem with food which is ruining their lives, whether it is because they are too fat, too thin, or just find food difficult. This book is an attempt to prevent this for future generations. The modern world makes it very easy to become fat and hard to stay healthy. I hope that this book has offered some useful ways to manage this without making food into a problem. Feeding your children unhealthy food is not great. But giving them a problem with food for the rest of their lives is far, far worse.

Recommended reading

Here are some books and websites that you might find useful.

Books

Bryant-Waugh, R. and Lask, B. 2013. *Eating Disorders: A Parents' Guide*. 2nd edn. London: Routledge.

Hunt, C. and Mountford, A. 2003. *The Parenting Puzzle. The Family Links Nurturing Programme*. Oxford: Family Links.

Ogden, J. 1992. *Fat Chance! The Myth of Dieting Explained*. London: Routledge. Translated into Portuguese (1993).

Ogden, J. 2010. *The Psychology of Eating: From Healthy to Disordered Behavior*. 2nd edn. Malden, MA: Wiley Blackwell.

Ogden, J. and Hills, L. 2008. Understanding sustained changes in behaviour: the role of life events and the process of reinvention. *Health: An International Journal*, 12, 419–437.

Treasure, J. and Alexander, J. 2013. *Anorexia Nervosa: A Recovery Guide for Sufferers, Families and Friends*. London: Routledge.

Websites

Allergy Action: the anaphylaxis campaign for people with food allergies (UK-based): http://allergyaction.org/

BEAT: charity for people with eating disorders offering advice and support: http://www.b-eat.co.uk/

FARE: the food allergy network (US-based): http://www.foodallergy.org/

Mumsnet: by parents for parents: http://www.mumsnet.com/

The NCT online support group: http://www.nct.org.uk/

References

1. Burnett, J. 1989. *Plenty and Want: A Social History of Food in England from 1815 to the Present Day*, 3rd edn. London: Routledge.
2. Department of Health 1991. *Dietary Reference Values for Food Energy and Nutrients for the United Kingdom*. Report on Health and Social Subjects, no. 41. London: HMSO.
3. Kelder, S.H., Perry, C.L., Klepp, K.-I., and Lytle, L.L. 1994. Longitudinal tracking of adolescent smoking, physical activity, and food choice behaviors. *American Journal of Public Health*, 84, 1121–1126.
4. Nicklas, T.A. 1995. Dietary studies of children and young adults (1973–1988): the Bogalusa heart study. *American Journal of Medical Science*, 310 (Suppl. 1), S101–S108.
5. Barker, D.J.P. (ed.) 1992. *Fetal and Infant Origins of Adult Disease*. London: BMJ Books.
6. Buttriss, J. 1995. *Nutrition in General Practice*, vol. 2: *Promoting Health and Preventing Disease*. London: Royal College of General Practitioners.
7. Wardle, J., Volz, C., and Golding, C. 1995. Social variation in attitudes to obesity in children. *International Journal of Obesity*, 19, 562–569.
8. Wardle, J., Steptoe, A., Bellisle, F., Davou, B., Reschke, K., Lappalainen, R., and Fredrikson, M. 1997. Health dietary practices among European students. *Health Psychology*, 16, 443–450.
9. Food Standards Agency and Department of Health. 2000–2001. National Diet and Nutrition Survey. Colchester: UK Data Archive. http://www.data-archive.ac.uk (accessed August 8, 2009).
10. Desor, J.A., Maller, O., and Turner, R.E. 1973. Taste and acceptance of sugars by human infants. *Journal of Comparative and Physiological Psychology*, 84, 496–501.

The Good Parenting Food Guide: Managing What Children Eat without Making Food a Problem, First Edition. Jane Ogden.
© 2014 John Wiley & Sons, Ltd. Published 2014 by John Wiley & Sons, Ltd.

11. Duncker, K. 1938. Experimental modification of children's food preferences through social suggestion. *Journal of Abnormal Social Psychology*, 33, 489–507.

12. Birch, L.L. 1980. Effects of peer models' food choices and eating behaviors on preschoolers' food preferences. *Child Development*, 51, 489–496.

13. Lowe, C.F., Dowey, A., and Horne, P. 1998. Changing what children eat. In A. Murcott (ed.), *The Nation's Diet: The Social Science of Food Choice*. London: Longman, 57–80.

14. Lepper, M., Sagotsky, G., Dafoe, J.L., and Greene, D. 1982. Consequences of superfluous social constraints: effects on young children's social inferences and subsequent intrinsic interest. *Journal of Personality and Social Psychology*, 42, 51–65.

15. Todhunter, E.N. 1973. Food habits, food faddism and nutrition. In M. Rechcigl (ed.), *Food, Nutrition and Health: World Review of Nutrition and Dietetics*, 16. Basel: Karger, 186–317.

16. Bruch, H. 1985. Four decades of eating disorders. In D.M. Garner and P.E. Garfinkel (eds.), *Handbook of Psychotherapy for Anorexia Nervosa and Bulimia*. New York: Guilford Press.

17. Lawrence, M. 1984. *The Anorexic Experience*. London: Women's Press.

18. Orbach, S. 1978. *Fat Is a Feminist Issue . . . How to Lose Weight Permanently – without Dieting*. London: Arrow Books.

19. Chernin, K. 1992. Confessions of an eater. In D.W. Curtin and L.M. Heldke (eds.), *Cooking, Eating, Thinking: Transformative Philosophies of Food*. Indianapolis: Indiana University Press, 56–67.

20. Levine, M.J. 1997. *I Wish I Were Thin, I Wish I Were Fat*. New York: Fireside.

21. Gordon, R.A. 2000. *Eating Disorders: Anatomy of a Social Epidemic*, 2nd edn. Oxford: Blackwell.

22. Crisp, A.H. 1984. The psychopathology of anorexia nervosa: getting the "heat" out of the system. In A.J. Stunkard and E. Stellar (eds.), *Eating and Its Disorders*. New York: Raven Press, 209–234.

23. Fiddes, N. 1990. *Meat: A Natural Symbol*. London: Routledge.

24. Funatogawa, I., Funatogawa, T., and Yano, E. 2008. Do overweight children necessarily make overweight adults? Repeated cross sectional annual nationwide survey of Japanese girls and women over nearly six decades. *British Medical Journal*, 337, a802.

25. Wardle, J., Brodersen, N.H., Cole, T.J., Jarvis, M.J., and Boniface, D.R. 2006. Development of adiposity in adolescence: five year longitudinal study of an ethnically and socioeconomically diverse sample of young people in Britain. *British Medical Journal*, 332, 1130–1135.

26. Baird, J., Fisher, D., Lucas, P., Kleijnen, J., Roberts, H., and Law, C. 2005. Being big or growing fast: systematic review of size and growth in infancy and later obesity. *British Medical Journal*, 331, 929.

27. Lerner, R.M. and Gellert, E. 1969. Body build identification, preference and aversion in children. *Developmental Psychology*, 1, 456–462.
28. Wadden, T.A. and Stunkard, A.J. 1985. Social and psychological consequences of obesity. *Annals of Internal Medicine*, 103, 1062–1067.
29. Mvo, Z., Dick, J., and Steyn, K. 1999. Perceptions of overweight African women about acceptable body size of women and children. *Curationis*, 22, 27–31.
30. Rothblum, E. 1990. Women and weight: fad and fiction. *Journal of Psychology*, 124, 5–24.
31. Kasen, S., Cohen, P., Chen, H., and Must, A. 2008. Obesity and psychopathology in women: a three decade prospective study. *International Journal of Obesity*, 32(3), 558–566.
32. Rand, C.S.W. and McGregor, A.M.C. 1991. Successful weight loss following obesity surgery and the perceived liability of morbid obesity. *International Journal of Obesity*, 15, 577–579.
33. Bullen, B.A., Reed, R.B., and Mayer, J. 1964. Physical activity of obese and non-obese adolescent girls appraised by motion picture sampling. *American Journal of Clinical Nutrition*, 4, 211–233.
34. Misra, A. and Ganda, O.P. 2007. Migration and its impact on adiposity and type 2 diabetes. *Nutrition*, 23(9), 696–708.
35. Christakis, N.A. and Fowler, J.H. 2007. The spread of obesity in a large social network over 32 years. *New England Journal of Medicine*, 357(4), 370–379.
36. Hill, J.O. and Peters, J.C. 1998. Environmental contributions to the obesity epidemic. *Science*, 280(5368), 1371–1374.
37. Prentice, A. 1999. Aetiology of obesity I: introduction. In *Obesity: The Report of the British Nutrition Foundation Task Force*. Oxford: Blackwell Science, 37–38.
38. Ogden, J., Coop, N., Cousins, C., Crump, R., Field, L., Hughes, S., and Woodger, N. 2013. Distraction, the desire to eat and food intake: towards an expanded model of mindless eating. *Appetite*, 62, 119–126.
39. Jebb, S.A., Prentice, A.M., Goldberg, G.R., Murgatroyd, P.R., Black, A.E., and Coward, W.A. 1996. Changes in macronutrient balance during over feeding and under feeding assessed by 12 day continuous whole body calorimetry. *American Journal of Clinical Nutrition*, 64, 259–266.
40. Laessle, R.G., Lehrke, S., and Dückers, S. 2007. Laboratory eating behavior in obesity. *Appetite*, 49, 399–404.
41. Bolton-Smith, C. and Woodward, M. 1994. Dietary composition and fat to sugar ratios in relation to obesity. *International Journal of Obesity*, 18, 820–828.
42. Blundell, J.E. and Macdiarmid, J. 1997. Fat as a risk factor for over consumption: satiation, satiety and patterns of eating. *Journal of the American Dietetic Association*, 97, 563–569.

43. Prentice, A.M. and Jebb, S.A. 1995. Obesity in Britain: gluttony or sloth? *British Medical Journal*, 311, 437–439.
44. Rissanen, A.M., Heliovaara, M., Knekt, P., Reunanen, A., and Aromaa, A. 1991. Determinants of weight gain and overweight in adult Finns. *European Journal of Clinical Nutrition*, 45, 419–430.
45. Waller, K., Kaprio, J., and Kujala, U.M. 2008. Associations between long-term physical activity, waist circumference and weight gain: a 30-year longitudinal twin study. *International Journal of Obesity*, 32(2), 353–361.
46. Shenassa, E.D., Frye, M., Braubach, M., and Daskalakis, C. 2008. Routine stair climbing in place of residence and Body Mass Index: a Pan-European population based study. *International Journal of Obesity*, 32(3), 490–494.
47. Hirsch, J. 1998. Magic bullet for obesity. *British Medical Journal*, 317, 1136–1138.
48. Ogden, J. and Sidhu, S. 2006. Adherence, behaviour change and visualisation: a qualitative study of patients' experiences of obesity medication. *Journal of Psychosomatic Research*, 61, 545–552.
49. Torgerson, J.S. and Sjostrom, L. 2001. The Swedish Obese Subjects (SOS) study – rationale and results. *International Journal of Obesity*, 35, S2–S4.
50. Ogden, J., Clementi, C., and Aylwin, S. 2006. Having obesity surgery: a qualitative study and the paradox of control. *Psychology and Health*, 21, 273–293.
51. Shute, J. 1992. *Life-size*. London: Mandarin.
52. Harbottle, E.J., Birmingham, C.L., and Sayani, F. 2008. Anorexia nervosa: a survival analysis. *Eating and Weight Disorders*, 21(5), 495–498.
53. Russell, G.F.M. 1979. Bulimia nervosa: an aminous variant of anorexia nervosa. *Psychological Medicine*, 9, 429–448.
54. Favaro, A. and Santonastaso, P. 1997. Suicidality in bulimia nervosa: clinical and psychological correlates. *Acta Psychiatrica Scandinavica*, 95, 508–514.
55. Tiggemann, M. 2006. The role of media exposure in adolescent girls' body dissatisfaction and drive for thinness: prospective results. *Journal of Social and Clinical Psychology*, 25(5), 523–541.
56. Ogden, J. and Mundray, K. 1996. The effect of the media on body satisfaction: the role of gender and size. *European Eating Disorders Review*, 4, 171–182.
57. Ogden, J. and Sherwood, F. 2009. Reducing the impact of media images: an evaluation of the effectiveness of an airbrushing educational intervention on body dissatisfaction. *Health Education*, 108, 489–500.
58. Wegner, D.M., Schneider, D.J., Cater, S.R. III, and White, T.L. 1987. Paradoxical effects of thought suppression. *Journal of Personality and Social Psychology*, 53, 5–13.
59. Connors, M.E. and Morse, W. 1993. Sexual abuse and eating disorders: a review. *International Journal of Eating Disorders*, 13, 1–11.

60. Feldman, M.B. and Meyer, I.H. 2007. Childhood abuse and eating disorders in gay and bisexual men. *International Journal of Eating Disorders*, 40(5), 418–423.
61. Treasure, J., Todd, G., and Szmukler, G.I. 1995. The inpatient treatment of anorexia nervosa. In G. Szmukler, C. Dare, and J. Treasure (eds.), *Handbook of Eating Disorders: Theory, Treatment and Research*. London: Wiley, 275–291.

Index

The Good Parenting Food Guide: Managing What Children Eat without Making Food a Problem, First Edition. Jane Ogden.
© 2014 John Wiley & Sons, Ltd. Published 2014 by John Wiley & Sons, Ltd.

This index was prepared by Neil Manley.